T0322629

To My Sisters

To My Sisters

A GUIDE TO BUILDING
LIFELONG FRIENDSHIPS

COURTNEY DANIELLA BOATENG
AND RENÉE KAPUKU

bluebird
books for life

First published 2023 by Bluebird
an imprint of Pan Macmillan
The Smithson, 6 Briset Street, London EC1M 5NR
EU representative: Macmillan Publishers Ireland Ltd, 1st Floor,
The Liffey Trust Centre, 117–126 Sheriff Street Upper,
Dublin 1, D01 YC43
Associated companies throughout the world
www.panmacmillan.com

ISBN 978-1-0350-0572-7 HB

1 3 5 7 9 8 6 4 2

A CIP catalogue record for this book is available from the British Library.

Typeset by Palimpsest Book Production Ltd, Falkirk, Stirlingshire
Printed and bound by CPI Group (UK) Ltd, Croydon, CR0 4YY

Visit **www.panmacmillan.com** to read more about all our books
and to buy them. You will also find features, author interviews and
news of any author events, and you can sign up for e-newsletters
so that you're always first to hear about our new releases.

COURTNEY
*To my sister Mary-Jo, your love,
forgiveness and friendship saved my life.
Thank you.*

RENÉE
*To my mother, whose strength, sacrifice and
unyielding prayers became the foundations
of the woman I am today.*

Contents

A Letter to Our Sisters

DEAR SISTER . . .

This is for you.

In fact, this entire book is for you.

Chances are, if you've picked up this little number, you're interested in trying to improve your relationships. Or perhaps you were gifted this by a sister, friend, colleague, spouse or someone in your circle who thinks you might enjoy or benefit from this. Or maybe you are simply curious to learn more about yourself.

Our plan is to help with all of the above. We know *everyone* wants to believe that their book will be transformational. But whilst that's what we hope, what we really need for that to be made a reality, is *you*. To get the most out of this book, we need your genuine engagement and open-mindedness.

Some of the themes and topics that are going to be discussed here may be sensitive and triggering to some. As your sisters, we encourage you to take care of yourself throughout the process. You might not finish it in one go, or you might find yourself coming back to the points that really resonate with you. Do whatever feels comfortable and right for you. Your journey through this book won't necessarily be easy, but hopefully it'll encompass real introspection, fulfilment and embracing of your innate personal agency.

Now that you've cracked open this book, to us, *you're a sister.* Welcome to the family.

WHO WE ARE

To My Sisters is a community-focused and community-led movement to help women across the globe become the best version of themselves – through the power of sisterhood. We started creating content to share our journey and to create a space for women to feel ownership over the conversations around womanhood and their human experience. What initially began as a podcast quickly spiralled into an online show, a thriving community of over a hundred thousand women, and multiple in-person and digital events all geared towards helping women find, and become, better people. TMS is an opportunity for us to create the biggest global sisterhood in existence and use female friendship to help support and empower women in their most audacious pursuits – providing educational opportunities, resources for making impact and tools to support inner healing.

At least, that's our big-picture, official vision. Underpinning all of these aims is a desire to create intimate comfortable spaces for women to be themselves. It's the biggest girls' gathering you've ever seen. Over at TMS, you can kick off your shoes, wear your comfiest attire, and bring *all* the tea and biscuits. Maybe some wine too, for good measure. It's always one of *those* evenings round here, where you don't have to show up as your best self but you'll certainly leave feeling as though you're somehow one step closer to being it.

This sisterhood began with our sisterhood – a friendship that spans over a decade and has gone through all the bumps, lumps and everything in between. We both grew up on council estates in London, both to first-generation immigrant parents who chose the United Kingdom as the place where they could try to make a decent living for their families. In the midst of difficult times, one of the most important things that saw a young Courtney and Renée through the simultaneously bleak and defining coming-of-age seasons was our friendship. We have survived traumatic experiences and gone on to thrive – building communities that matter and sparking change for women across the world.

Along the way, we've made some amazing life choices, as well as some detrimental ones too. We've made excellent friends and we've had our fair share of traumatizing platonic experiences. In the great 'aha' moments and the more stressful 'oh no!' exclamations, we always had each other to depend on. Both of us also have the shared experience of being the eldest daughter in our households, so parentification, early maturation, and the necessity of taking up mantles that were never ours is something we know all too well (we'll be talking about these things in depth in later chapters). It is in this spirit that we'd always wanted to write something tangible and solid – not just for each other, or for our sisters and friends – but for you, who can most likely relate to the complexities of life as a woman, and as a friend or sister to those who are closest to you.

A couple of disclaimers, sis. We are writing this from the perspective of people who are growing. We don't claim to be perfect, or the cream of the crop, or experts with decades of experience. We're drawing on our own glowing and growing journey, a friendship that has spanned over a decade and a commitment to getting better every single day. We're constantly being shaped by each other, by the women closest to us and by the ever-growing TMS community. We aren't showing you what to do, or how to act, or who to be. We're giving you guidance, in real time, based on our experience and learnings. We're on a path, same as you. The only difference is we're choosing to share some crafty bits and pieces we believe may help you too, and we've decided to do it together.

We're walking right beside you.

We've been through the highs and lows of life and relationships. We've experienced great pain and suffering, but this has also been paired with incredible achievements and such wonderful experiences. We bring all of this together in this book but, most importantly, we share the tips, tricks and wisdom we've picked up along the way. The things so often left unsaid, the things we wished we'd known and the things we'd love you to know as you embark on your own journey.

THE SISTERHOOD REVOLUTION

The time for what we call the 'sisterhood revolution' is now. Women are making incredible strides across fields and industries, redefining what womanhood means and pushing the boundaries of what we have previously normalised as possible. We're seeing women climb to the highest rungs of the corporate ladder, start organisations, pioneer in education, create meaningful products, produce mass content and engage in social, political movements. Using the tools of the future – technology and the internet – women are leveraging implicit collective thinking to achieve unimaginable things.

This guide has been written on the cusp of such greatness. It's an opportunity to reflect deeply in collective, structural, interpersonal and individual ways about how we can create and maintain these bonds we have with each other. Collective – through gathering our resources to support other women in their quest to win. Structural – as we can use this as an opportunity to challenge social narratives about womanhood that have left us out of the equation. Interpersonal – in changing the way we relate to one another for the better. And individual – as by becoming better people, we become better women. This is our multi-pronged approach to creating the space for women to win, through building communities for women, by women.

If you need another reason why the sisterhood revolution is necessary, it's this: we were made for the community. Human beings need personal connections with other human beings. Despite the fact that we are all so hyper-connected by the digital world, we are seeing mental health crises skyrocket and conversations on wellbeing for women crop up again and again. How did we become so connected and yet so lonely? A study by the CDC showed that loneliness and social isolation can negatively impact our physical and mental wellbeing, leading to increased risks of depression, anxiety, heart disease, stroke and even premature death. It's no exaggeration to state that we *need* other people.

There's also something decidedly special about female friendships. Quite a large proportion of the latest research on stress and stress responses has focused on men. For a long time, scientists believed that the primary response in the face of fear, stress and difficult situations was the fight or flight response. However, more recent work by UCLA suggests that women have a much larger behavioural range in response, with one those being termed 'tending and befriending' by a National Library of Medicine study. Essentially, in times of stress, we need to gather up communities and turn to other women for comfort, support and general wellbeing. A study published in the *Psychology of Women Quarterly* showed that there is a perceived therapeutic value of friendship between women. Now, this isn't to say you should start seeing your gal pals as your new therapist but it does go to show the specific function and necessity of cultivating friends as women, *with women*, goes far beyond something that's simply nice to do.

It's something you need.

In our own experiences, our female friendships have been nothing short of transformative. We've been lucky enough to have each other, as sisters, to draw from. We've also been lucky enough to have a wealth of women in our circle, who you will come to meet throughout this book, to share our journey of life with. However, as great as they all have been, we've been busy trying our hand at recruiting more women for the movement, and as it so happens, *you* were on our mind.

Are you ready to step into the frontline of our revolution?

Don't worry – we won't let you step out alone.

SHARING OUR SOULS WITH OUR SISTERS

You probably have a plethora of books on the shelf filled with detailed advice and blueprints on how to become a better person or lead a better life. As women, we can find ourselves bombarded with endless content that has us picking apart our mindset, habits and beliefs in the hope that by mastering certain tools, we can become the healthiest, happiest and most productive versions of ourselves. We will be the first to admit that it can get exhausting. We have found ourselves letting out heavy sighs as we discover a new video or podcast trying to dictate to us who we, as women, should or should not be; how we should act, what we should think and what the epitome of femininity is. This guide does not exist to tell you that you're not good enough or tear you apart for not being the perfect person or friend. This book is a map for those of us who admit to being works in progress.

Take your time with this book, sis. Chew on the words and mull over every reflection at your own pace. Littered across these pages are our innermost thoughts, fears and discoveries. Revelations birthed out of the testing of our characters and shaped by the observation and identification of patterns and principles that regularly pop up in the stories of women we interact with. Our stories aren't always pretty – they speak of the growing pains that come with evolution. In the course of our decade-long friendship, we have seen each other mature, evolve and handle transition. We can both say confidently that the process is not perfect, nor is it comfortable. With as much change as we have witnessed, we know that there is so much more change to come in the future, from marriage to motherhood, ageing and bereavement. We want to create systems and mindsets that can handle these new seasons well. To create a culture of sisterhood that can withstand the tides of change.

We are not perfect and we are not your blueprint, we are just one of many examples. In a society that holds women to unreachable standards, we seek for sisterhood to be a space where women are liberated from the crippling pressure that comes with trying to live up to static, unyielding images of femininity. We believe that one of the ways this can happen is through women using transparency to build intimacy – being bold enough to take off the mask and admit their struggles. We're here to let you know that failure is normal but it's not final. Give yourself and your sisters the grace to get up and try again because we all need a chance to do better once we know better. Sisterhood is your safe space to try and try again – thriving once you've mastered it.

These intimate spaces that sisterhood creates are ones in which we are not only held accountable but we are also celebrated loudly. As you read this book, take time to identify the things that you get right and should continue to do, but also use it as an opportunity to give your friends their flowers. Highlight the great contribution your friends have brought to your life, as well as the amazing qualities that they have. Make it a priority to focus on their positive achievements and what milestones you have reached as friends.

You should also use this book as a chance to recognise your progress as you complete the tasks and reflect on the changes you make as you mature. You deserve to be praised and to remember how far you have come – not only in your relationships but also in your personal development journey. We wish you nothing but success on this journey of self-improvement and finding true and authentic friendship. Your wins are our wins and we have made it our personal mission to see women win in all areas of life.

But as much as we aim to inspire you and will cheer you along, the real work begins when you close this book and spend time with your friends, colleagues, classmates and family members. Do not do this work alone. Our charge to you, sis, is to be bold enough to read and complete this book in community. Encourage the women around you to read it as you do, or maybe even after you complete it, and discuss the topics we present to you. Ask them to share their insights and perspectives with you. Use this book as a starting point for deep conversations, opportunities to share and listen. We are happy to break the ice for you, to get past the social awkwardness that precedes vulnerability by putting our business out there first, but once we open that door, we ask that you walk through it and share your story with the women in your life.

WHAT TO EXPECT FROM THIS BOOK

This isn't a self-help book – it's an 'us' help book. The topics of discussion start within the pages of this book but we want you to take them to your sisters. You may even find that you disagree with us! Diversity of thought is always welcome, so please share your thoughts with us by engaging with us across our social media platforms @tomysisterhood.

This guide will challenge you to be brave enough to be vulnerable with other people and yourself without shame. Fear of vulnerability can make us settle and compromise for surface-level relationships, where you don't feel you can share the full picture of what was and is happening in your life and on your life journey. You know, the kind of relationships where the answer to 'how are you?' is never how you honestly feel but rather a generic, socially accepted response that doesn't make anyone uncomfortable. Throughout this book, we'll be equipping you with the vocabulary and tools needed to understand, dismantle and rebuild your relationships, so that they are fruitful and meaningful, and far more than skin deep.

These chapters are as practical as they are poetic, so grab a notepad, a pen and a highlighter. At the end of the chapters, you will find activities that you can do both alone and with your friends to help you master the tools we have discussed and grow in the areas you have read about. From setting your own dreams and goals, to outlining what you desire from your intimate relationships and identifying where you are being underserved, we're going to equip you with language and strategy to express and assess yourself and others.

Like any other relationship, friendships require work; there's a lot beneath the surface. This book is a toolkit for exploring how you and your friends deal with various issues, confronting your behaviour and asking how it could be impacting your ability to find, make and keep lifelong friendships. And in every toolkit there must be tools. These will be key in assisting you to become self-aware in knowing who you are, who your real friends are and how you can become a better friend based on your awareness of their needs.

Use this book as a mirror to help you see yourself for who you currently are. See it as an open door to who you could be. Search your soul and connect to your true feelings towards yourself and the people around you, even if that means unpacking feelings which are uncomfortable.

Ultimately, as every author does, we have huge ambitions and hopes for this book. But our greatest desire is that it will cause you to search for and embrace the love that sisterhood provides. That you will flourish under the nurturing of that love. And that you will overflow in it.

Love,

Renée and Courtney

CHAPTER 1

We All Need a Sister, Sis

Our Sisterhood Journey and What's to Come

*'The fountain of my joy cannot come from
one place, I drink from many wells.'*
COURTNEY

Courtney

*We were both good at hiding our true emotions behind poker faces;
Renée even more so than me. But that moment she took hold of my
tear-covered hands, hands as heavy as the burdens I was carrying
on my shoulders, and she looked at me with tears falling from her
eyes too, I realised, she saw me for what I truly was. Broken. It
was this feeling that made me sob and run out of that classroom.
It was the first time she had seen me cry and, now she had witnessed
this, there was no need for me to resume any act. I didn't need to be
the vibrant Courtney she sat next to in English and history. Instead,
she told me we would fix these broken pieces 'together'. That's when
I knew Renée wasn't just a friend, she was a sister.*

• • •

We'll get back to this story in a minute.

First things first, this book isn't just a tale of our friendships,
it's a guide to help you build real sisterhood in your life, because

we know from first-hand experience that life is not meant to be done alone, sis! However, in order for us to build healthy friendships, community and sisterhood that are more than superficial, we must first confront the ideas we hold about independence. The narrative of the modern-day woman is one centred around self-sufficiency. We are learning to become self-focused in our growth and development. This isn't necessarily a bad thing – we need self-awareness, internal motivation and the ability to hold ourselves accountable in order to succeed in becoming the best versions of ourselves. This is what helps us to become strong individuals, ready to run the race of life, face its obstacles and get closer to achieving our wildest dreams; particularly when no one else believes in us and we have to do it alone.

But whilst we may be working *on* ourselves, we are not *by* ourselves and, if we believe that the personal growth journey is about cultivating hyper-independence in our endeavour to transformation, we will not put to use one of the greatest resources we have in our lives – those around us. Our friends, family and mentors perceive us in a way we are unable to. They notice our blind spots and can sometimes even appreciate us in a better light than our insecurities, fears and imposter syndrome would allow us to.

A lot of us have colleagues, acquaintances and even people who we consider to be friends who we encounter often, but who we may not have invited to 'do life' with us. They are alongside us as we continue on our lone journeys. But when it comes to those friends with whom we 'click', the people we choose to make family, we have to challenge ourselves to do the work of creating a culture of trust and vulnerability so that those relationships can flourish. These are relationships and connections we cannot survive without.

Everyone needs someone to love, support and cherish them unconditionally, in spite of their performance. And this doesn't always take the form of a spouse or a parent. What if in that feeling of loneliness, or in that craving for deep connection, love and support, what we need isn't romance but simply a good ol' sister? A friend to *do life* with.

LONELINESS

It's a feeling many of us don't want to admit we have. Or that, for a lot of us, we don't even recognise we're experiencing. We just know that we would appreciate having someone to talk to, be in the presence of and experience things with. Many progressive societies encourage a false impression that we don't need anyone, but this over-reliance on the self can leave us lonely and yet unable to pinpoint the lingering sensation of emptiness in our lives and schedules. Let's be honest, it can show up most prominently when we're single. How often do we tell ourselves that the remedy to our loneliness would be getting into a relationship? Becoming the object of someone's affection and attention. Encompassing 'baecations', dinner dates and enjoying quality time, a romantic relationship will surely fill the void? So we spend our time daydreaming about what our next romance will look like, improving ourselves in preparation for 'the one' and arranging the things in our life to make way for love.

There is a slight obsession with romantic relationships in today's society. Whether through social media, in films or even our own cultural experiences, society is constantly communicating to us, in particular, as women, that within these patriarchal systems there's a level of happiness, success and value that is only unlocked by being in a long-term committed relationship with a man. We've found from personal experience and from the sisters in the TMS community that this is a message many of us have internalised; despite being 'modern-day women' who are excelling in varying spheres, many of us fear 'being alone forever'. And whilst we could talk for hours about the many shortcomings of the patriarchal system or teach you about connecting with yourself and enjoying your singleness instead, the real issue here is that companionship, trust and love have become synonymous with romance. Even married couples can attest to the need for community and friendship outside of a romantic relationship.

Have we become so obsessed with romance that we have forgotten how to build connection through true friendships? Do we only know how to have intimacy through sex? Are we reserving unconditional love for our partners and denying the people around us the support they need from us as we focus our energy on maintaining the form of love we think is the most important? Are we denying ourselves different experiences of love in our life because we think it can only come from one place?

Don't get us wrong – we believe in healthy and flourishing romantic relationships and that they should be pursued and enjoyed – but making meaningful connections isn't exclusive to romance. Within romantic relationships, we challenge ourselves to do the work of developing personally, healing from trauma and establishing boundaries because we don't want to harm the person we love, but we must do the same in our platonic friendships if we don't want to hurt our friends, who love us and support us.

When did life become so complicated, so much that we needed a book on something as simple as 'how to make good friends and be one'? Surely it's not that hard, given we all have female friends? Women we grew up with, went to school with, work with and probably even live with. But being around people doesn't mean you're truly connecting, and knowing someone

isn't the same as trusting them. The words you read and activities you'll complete as you make your way through this book
are here to help you with this, and to make the idea of finding
and maintaining these deep connections less intimidating.

THE FALLACY OF MODERN 'COMMUNITIES'

It's easy to connect with people these days, right? It comes with
the tap of buttons that say 'follow', 'request' and 'subscribe'.
Upon doing so, we become invested in the lives of the people
we have connected with. They entertain us and their voices and
stories may even inspire us to change our lives. And we become
a part of communities who are interested in the same things we
are and possibly have the same goals. Heck, you may even be a
part of an online sisterhood where two women talk to you about
the wellness, growth and development of a community of sisters
across the world! It still confounds us that women are listening
to the podcast from almost every country in the world and yet
every episode still feels so intimate, like each sister is sat in the
room with us. We are so grateful for all you sisters in our digital
community, and our greatest desire for each of you is that you have
a community of sisters who you are connected with and influenced
by in real life. Let's be honest, once you come to the end of that
episode or video and you lock your phone screen or close your
laptop and look up, who's there to help you deal with those areas
in your life where you were 'triggered' by that episode you just
played or the caption you just read? Who is keeping you accountable to those goals you set? Who is there to help you celebrate your
milestones or recover from your failures?

You see, having access to a digital sisterhood community like
To My Sisters is amazing. We started it out of a hope for everyone

to experience life-changing, healthy friendships. The type that is so deep, even blood couldn't thicken it. However, the true magic of sisterhood is something we share as best friends that unfortunately we cannot have with everyone in our online community: intimacy. Whilst we can all take advice from the people we watch and listen to, whose opinions make us intro-spective, true accountability and vulnerability cannot happen without proximity. You need people who are close enough to you that they can identify who you truly are and what you really need. After all, anything can look good from afar but it's when we draw nearer that we see its true nature – flaws and all. To be intimate with someone is to allow them to *know* you, to gain an understanding of who you are and become acquainted with the private side of you that few people gain access to.

These days, the word 'community' is overused. From brand marketing to workplace culture, it's often used in an attempt to foster a sense of togetherness and solidarity. Yet we are living in a time where people feel the most disconnected, lonely and anxious. You've probably heard the saying 'it takes a village to raise a child', and it's something that we experienced growing up. We both saw our mothers lean on the 'aunties' in our families and communities. These were women who they were related to by blood or simply by experience. They would pick us up from school, bring us groceries and containers filled with rice when our mothers were dealing with the weight of their responsibilities, from late-night work shifts to family and financial troubles. We were raised by communities that prioritised the freedom to ask for help and know that you could find it in your friends.

But these women who made up our 'village' weren't always invited into every situation. As children of West African immi-grants, we grew up navigating and fusing two cultures. We would go to school and see posters advising us to call Childline if we were unsafe at home and return home to parents who believed physical discipline was a norm. We were warned to never 'air your dirty laundry' and that 'whatever happened at home, stayed at home'. Many of us may have internalised unwritten rules about vulnerability, weakness and honesty from our respective cultures and upbringings. Some of us may have learned that you don't admit weakness and you keep up appearances at all costs. It may sound extreme, but as working-class immigrants who had just left their homes to come to a new, foreign land with large cultural differences and less-than-favourable attitudes towards ethnic minorities, our parents had to be careful, cautious and independent. For some of our parents, or even some of us who have experienced a lack of basic living essentials, conver-sations around 'feelings' and 'trauma' can seem like a waste of precious time. Maybe you grew up in a family that feared the judgement of your neighbours, where you felt the pressure to 'keep up with the Joneses', or that you had to hide your struggles and challenges in order to maintain a false image of perfection.

No matter your upbringing, the way you were taught to navi-gate vulnerability or the way it was modelled to you when you were young will dictate how you approach building trust with others. If you grew up believing that people weren't to be trusted with the truth of who you really were behind closed doors, you probably learned to stay strong and silent. You may have become skilled in the art of putting on a brave face, or a mask. Never revealing when you were struggling mentally, financially or rela-tionally, out of fear that you'd be the subject of gossip or viewed through judging eyes. But until you admit you need it, how do you expect to find help?

If this is you, it'll probably surprise you when you find out you're not the only person struggling. But someone has to be the first to break through the silence and give everyone else the permission to admit that we all need support. It doesn't just take a village to raise a child, it also takes some villagers to help you not to lose your mind as you're trying to raise them. Whether you're a mother or not, you're nurturing something in your life. You may be trying to grow your finances, your career or even your character. That growth needs a village.

BUT WHY DO I NEED 'SISTERHOOD'?

Sisterhood with a big 'S'

'Sisterhood' is a word often used to describe women's solidarity. It's a term employed to rally women together and create an impression of oneness and support, especially in the fight against gender inequality. However, as with many phrases used across the academic, commercial and corporate worlds, it can become misused and somewhat of a cliché. As we embark on learning more about building authentic friendship and sisterhood, it is important for us to deconstruct this term, not only for what it means in our personal lives but also what it means politically.

'Sisterhood' has long been used in feminist rhetoric as one of the greatest devices women have in our arsenal in the fight against sexism, sexual violence and many other things that women fall victim to on a daily basis due to patriarchy. As we challenge ourselves to build authentic friendships with other women, we must contend with our beliefs about them. Patriarchy and the systems that enforce it have not only taught us how we are to relate to men but it has also dictated to us how we should or should not bond with women.

Growing up, many of us watched films, read books and had conversations with our families that trained us to believe that men are the 'prize' and that male approval is the measure of our 'success' in womanhood. This belief dictated much of our own behaviour, from the way we dressed to how we spoke. You might recall magazine articles or even YouTube videos sharing top tips to make yourself 'irresistible' or teaching you how to 'please' a man. Or you may have memories of a family member making you feel bad about the way you looked, suggesting it would make you 'unappealing' to men. Maybe you decided against pursuing a career in a certain field because it was deemed too masculine. Many of us have been there. Centuries of programming have led us to believe this is a 'man's world' in which a woman's place is to simply be an accessory, a perfectly constructed image to be gazed at and consumed. The majority of us globally find ourselves having internalised this idea.

There are, however, many women who have never bought into this sexist rhetoric, not only openly disagreeing with it but living in a way which defies such expectations and pressures. Such women often find themselves being called 'radical' or labelled 'feminists' as an insult. They are not only chastised but also ostracised by the men and women in their own lives. Whilst men are the oppressors and benefactors of these harmful structures, we have all to a degree internalised the unwritten rules of patriarchy, and thus people of any gender, orientation, class or creed can become complicit in enforcing them on a daily basis. Even if we profess to have embraced feminist discourse and that we all believe in 'equality for women', a main point in the to-do list to achieving true equality is all of us noticing and problematising the unconscious bias we have against women, even as women.

One of the biggest ways we can see this unconscious bias play out is in our treatment of other women as competition or a threat. That the women around us are an obstacle to our success, not only in finding a partner, but in our professional lives too. Fuelled by our fear of 'time running out' on our reproductive window, we are made to believe that men are scarce (the good ones, at least) and that we should compete with other women to capture their attention. Or that there can only be 'one woman at the top' in our professional field. These feelings of fear and scarcity lead to comparison, competition, jealousy and individualism.

These are also things which are sometimes associated with female friendships – that they are filled with cattiness, gossip and fakery. And as much as we believe wholeheartedly in the power of sisterhood, we cannot ignore that this is reflective of some women's female friendship experiences, and relationships can become toxic if we do not put in the effort to confront our internalised misogyny. But, be encouraged, we are here to tell you that there are women around you and all across the world who not only desire meaningful female friendship but are also willing to do the work of inspecting and challenging themselves in order to build it.

Sisterhood is as much about becoming a better person and a better friend as it is about unbecoming most of what society has told us as women to be. Unfortunately, society often illustrates women – and some more than others – as aggressive, dramatic, hysterical and generally unpleasant. Our job here isn't to suggest that women cannot be these things, but it is rather to challenge why we are so quick to give women these labels in the first place. We must come to the realisation that many of us have been programmed to believe it is not beneficial to have women as friends. Given that the approval of men is regarded as deter-mining our value, the pursuit of other women and their friendship can be perceived to be pointless (unless it is a tool for us to bond with men).

It would be easy to conclude here, as many feminist writers have, that, plainly and simply, 'sisterhood' as a political move-ment is the solution to many of these issues women face due to gender inequality. That our solidarity, as we metaphorically hold hands and braid each other's hair around a campfire, will give us the hope and comfort we need to continue on in this long fight against oppression. However, true sisterhood cannot be achieved until women also confront the inequality which exists amongst them. We must take an intersectional approach to sisterhood, or else it ceases to be sisterhood and is instead about the most privileged women taking centre stage, using 'othered' women as support for themselves, unaware that they have simply built another hierarchical structure in which they sit at the top, using their power to oppress, marginalise and render invisible the women who do not look like them or have their resources.

American author and activist bell hooks unpacks this in her writing, *Sisterhood: Political Solidarity Between Women*. She explains that we cannot band together as 'sisters' to fight against men as our common oppressor based just on the shared identity of being 'women'. What it means to be a woman and the day-to-day realities that come with that varies globally and culturally, with unique experiences emerging at the various intersections of gender with class, race, ethnicity, geography, sexuality, disability, religion and more. If we are to build true and authentic sisterhood in our personal lives and within the feminist movement, we must not only become aware of these differences in lived experiences but we must also honour them. We need to make it a priority to use our resources to support women in their fight against all forms of oppression by sharing our resources and knowledge. We as sisters cannot be gatekeepers to the little power that we may hold in our respective spheres – instead we must become gates to give women access to equip themselves better in these battles. This cannot be done by paying lip service, using sisterhood as a meaningless slogan and catchphrase, it must be done through sacrifice, the true cornerstone of revolution.

We must give all women the stage to share their story and be willing to identify and accept where we have occupied the role of the enemy in their lives by hindering them from achieving full freedom, safety and liberation. Our stories don't have to be made into films or published in books for them to be told or for them to be important. Our lives matter and are dignified purely because they are ours and they are true. They deserve to be told. Women so often feel as though they must be silent, that their words don't matter and their voices shouldn't be heard. Throughout this book, we will encourage you to have conversations with the women around you, both the easy and the hard ones. Sisterhood is a place where we are able to take the muzzle off of our mouths and are granted the privilege to be honest. It is the arena in which we not only have the freedom to tell our stories of pain and joy loudly, but where we come to listen attentively too.

FREEDOM TO BE VULNERABLE

Courtney

So, back to our friendship love story.

Renée and I had known each other since 2008 – we were 11 years old at the time – but we became best friends in 2014. We had just started our first year of sixth form and, unfortunately for me, all my secondary school friends had decided to go to other colleges, leaving me in need of an entirely new friendship circle. Fortunately, I didn't have to look too far. Back in secondary school, my friendship group would sit on a lunch table next to another group of six girls who were just as loud as us and laughed just as hard as we did. I decided that they would now be my new friends, and it was with that decision and in this new chapter of my life that I grew closer to a girl I had only known of up until that point as 'the smartest girl in school', Renée

Kapuku. We took a lot of the same classes, discovered we had similar ambitions and liked each other's humour – a simple shared glance could send us into hysterical laughter. To put it simply, we 'clicked'.

Renée and I came from similar low-socio-economic backgrounds but we were radical dreamers. We aimed for the best and it was on the grounds of this common tenacity for upward mobility and a desire for destiny fulfilled that we decided to help one another journey through academic life together. Being in an all-girls school, we had witnessed the stereotypes surrounding female friendships. How they could be drowned in jealousy, gossip, comparison and competition. At times, there was an ugliness that could make anyone swear off letting any woman get close to them ever again, but we had experienced a different reality in our friendship group. There was a warmth, love and empowerment that flowed endlessly there.

So we became 'best friends', but then, for me, our friendship transitioned into sisterhood at one pivotal moment in my life. Renée and I had always performed well at school (like I said, she was the smartest girl there!) and she had the grades to prove it. So, when choosing our next steps on our academic path, it was only right that we challenged ourselves. Our goal was to become two of the first in our school's history to receive admission into Oxford and Cambridge, the two most prestigious universities in the UK. But as we made that decision and entered our final year of sixth form, a year we were going to dedicate to making that vision and reality, my mum, a single parent, became sick with a life-threatening condition. This meant that for my family to survive, I had to take on some financial responsibility in my household.

Alongside studying full time and undertaking extra-curricular activities, I also had a job as a hair stylist after school – doing six-to-seven hour shifts, three days a week and six days a week during the holidays. It was brutal but I never told anyone how I truly felt about my situation. I accepted it as the cards I had been dealt; a burden no one else should have the responsibility of helping me carry because it was a test

*of my own strength and mental fortitude. So, I still showed up, still
made people laugh, gave people advice and tried to excel academically as
I prepared myself for the gruelling university application process. But I
could only keep up with the demands of my own life for so long.*

*Soon, I was tired all the time and my mental health was
deteriorating. My school attendance fell to 49 per cent and I could
feel my dreams and aspirations of going to Cambridge – along with
everyone's belief in my ability to do so – running away from me as
quickly as anxiety and panic were overwhelming me. One day, in an
English literature lesson, sitting next to Renée, sleep deprived and
becoming more and more aware of how much I didn't know and how
far behind I was compared to my class, tears began to fill my eyes and
hit my open workbook on the desk with almost as much heaviness as I
felt inside. I couldn't take it anymore. I ran out of the classroom, into
the toilets across the hallway and began to wail. That moment marked
a break in the veneer of strength I had been presenting to support my
mother through recovery and encourage my friends as they pursued
their own ambitions. Inside that strong exterior was the true
Courtney and she was alone, not only in that bathroom stall, but in
life, because no one knew the true her.*

*I heard the bathroom door open. It was Renée. She had come to
find me along with another friend and it was the first time she had
seen this side of me. I exhaled deeply and told her that whilst we had
both dreamed of and started the journey towards Oxbridge together, I
had decided I wasn't going to go to university; I needed to work and
help my family. She held my hands, looking at me with conviction
and loving firmness, and told me that she wasn't going to let me give
up on my happiness, that we would face whatever challenges I was
facing 'together'. It was the first time in my life that I truly felt seen
for what I was, outside of what I could do.*

•   •   •

Sometimes, the idea of letting someone come close enough that they see the real us can be frightening because we're scared that they won't just judge us; they'll also discover that we do not live up to the expectations and ideals they have for us and that we have set for ourselves. But after that moment, Renée went from being my friend to my sister. Rather than solely focusing on getting me out of that bathroom and back to reaching my goals, she was focused on helping me deal with the internal mental and emotional challenges I was going through. She wanted to make sure I was healing and whole whilst I was achieving. Our relationship was no longer based on what we could do, but who we were – the good, the bad and the ugly. This change in our relationship made us start asking each other tough questions and challenging each other to become better people. It meant we were all up in each other's business (with each other's permission, of course), looking past the superficial successes and victories. It made our friendship more intense but more rewarding because we now had someone to journey with, who loved us and who could see where we wanted to go in life but was more concerned by how we got there.

WHAT IS A SISTER?

There are many different types of relationships. From 'colleague' and 'acquaintance' to 'friend' and the coveted 'best friend' accolade, each of these titles come with different implications, responsibilities and privileges. Of these, the label that's thrown around the most is 'friend'. We use it to refer to many different people who have different levels of access to us. Social media can be partly to blame. From the inception of Facebook, with many social media sites following suit, you could add people to your network by sending them a 'friend request'. Of course, the original intention was that platforms like Facebook would be digital replicas of your real-life network; that only people who knew you offline would request to digitally befriend you. Do you remember when Facebook used to have a little disclaimer before you hit the 'request' button reminding you that you should only send requests to people you actually knew?

Nowadays, in the era of public profiles, we don't need to have an established in-person relationship with someone, or even a degree of familiarity, before we become digital 'friends' with them. We can simply choose to request to join their network because we think they look interesting or maybe we met them briefly and want to continue to connect. Either way, once they accept our request, we find ourselves in a list labelled 'friends'. It's no surprise that the word 'friend' is now so commonly used to refer to pretty much anyone we know.

We shouldn't be afraid of giving people different labels, depending on our relationship with them, as different relationships come with different expectations. We don't expect the same levels of support, loyalty and time from our colleagues as we do our friends. We know that they occupy different spaces in our lives. If a colleague didn't attend your birthday party, you probably wouldn't be upset. If your best friend failed to show up, your sadness or anger towards them would be warranted. Why? You've put greater expectations on them because they are 'closer' to you. Relationships are all about 'closeness'.

A 'sister' is probably one of the closest people in your life. We go to them in our greatest times of weakness and they are present in our happiest times of success, often having contributed to our victory. Whether blood related or not, the people we choose to call our best friends become our confidants based on the qualities they display and the way they interact with us.

Some defining characteristics of a sister:

- She's in your corner. Think of a boxing match: a sister watches you go toe-to-toe with life, taking its punches and dishing some out, too. When you come back to your corner of the ring, sometimes limping or filled with adrenaline, you take time to recover, get replenished and re-strategise. You should have a friend who is equipped to help you do all those things.

- She offers you support, a listening ear and a shoulder to cry on. She helps lighten the burden. You've heard the phrase, 'a problem shared is a problem half solved'. A close friend is there to help you face your problems. She is the first person we want to go to when things happen.

- She is a source of joy in your life. Much of life can be emotionally and mentally draining; our sisterhoods and intimate relationships are where we go to be refreshed.

- She's committed to doing the journey of life with you. We all go through different seasons of life, evolving as we are presented with challenges, reach new milestones and adopt the various hats and titles womanhood can bestow on us. A sister stands by your side, helping you adjust to the environment.

- She's invested in your holistic wellness, sharing her resources, time, energy and presence.

- She is a great influence in your life. She inspires you and her words share approval or disapproval.

- She sees the best in you, even when you cannot see it for yourself. She will speak life into you and your vision by encouraging and reminding you how great you are, and how much potential is in you.

- A sister is a challenger. She teaches you more about yourself and stretches you to love yourself, her and others well.
- She holds you accountable, reminding you of the standards you've set yourself and the goals you've vocalised. She is unafraid of telling you the truth.
- A sister loves you. A lot of us have different definitions of what love is but there should be no doubt that the friends you put the title 'sister' on love you.

Feel free to add to this list what you expect from a close friend. Friendships and relationships are all about expectation. Some of us enter into friendships and relationships afraid of disappointment, so we don't lay out any rules because we believe it to be the best way to stop people from failing us. But this is a guaranteed way to hold yourself back from experiencing the joy that comes with having your needs met. How else will we measure if and how we are truly cared about if we do not set and express our wants? Having expectations of your friends is necessary. Find out what yours are and be confident in expressing them, in order to give your friends the opportunity to meet them.

LET'S FIND AND BUILD YOUR LIFELONG FRIENDSHIPS

Sometimes, we engage in friendships which do not hold a mirror up to us, hold us accountable or call us out on our bad behaviour. We turn to entertaining company with those who will only praise us. Or, as we spend more time glued to our phones, consuming content and building social media platforms, we become deceived into thinking of our online friends as our real friends. These friendships can bring value but it is important to make a conscious effort to invest in real-life encounters, experiences and relationships. We are sure most of us can admit to engaging in endless scrolling through our vibrant social media timelines sometimes as a pacifier to the truth – that we feel lonely, bored or isolated in our real lives.

Don't get us wrong, surface-level relationships aren't bad, they have their place and we're certainly not telling you to go up to people at professional networking events and try to find out their deepest, darkest secrets and fears! But you need a few friends who have access to the true you and not just the 'you' you present outwardly so people will accept you. These are friendships where you're not afraid to share the truth of who you are or to get your hands dirty helping each other through tough times. This is something that cannot, and more importantly should not, be done with one-sided relationship dynamics, because vulnerability requires reciprocity so we can comfortably build trust.

DISCLAIMER, IT'S GOING TO GET DEEP

We are your sisters and when it comes to sisterhood, things can get *real deep, real quick*. So this is a warning – we will be in your business in this book. But we will be putting our business out there too because, like we've mentioned before, in order to build friendship, vulnerability has to be reciprocal. Throughout our friendship and individual journeys of self-growth, we have had to acknowledge our pasts and characteristics, especially within our relationship. Sometimes confronting those harsh realities has been, quite frankly, uncomfortable. But growth isn't comfortable and we can testify

that beauty often starts out awkward too. It's worth the investment of digging deep into parts of ourselves we may have
hidden and haven't discovered yet.

It's easy to expect a lot from the people that come into our
lives. We rightfully want people to value, love and support us
unconditionally, but we won't know the true value of such
precious treatment if we don't first learn what it takes to give
it. Being a good friend can seem easy but human beings are
complicated. We come with a history of experiences, learnt
behaviours and responses which form our personalities. We
expect people to accept us as we are because it's all we've ever
known ourselves to be, but if we want to have healthy friendships,
to be interdependent and experience true community, we must
first look inwards at what might be stopping us from having
what we desire. It'll take time, so be patient with yourself as
you discover new things. This experience may deliver a few
blows but remember, we're growing together.

Over the course of these chapters, we're going to cover eight
areas that will help you find and build real, lifelong friendships
on your sisterhood journey.

1. Learning what kind of friend you are

We don't all face the same challenges when it comes to being
in friendships. For example, some people find it easier to be
vulnerable and welcome people's help, whilst others cringe at
the idea of making their needs known. In the next chapter, we
will describe five friendship profiles you might relate to. The
aim of this is two-fold: to help you identify the things you do
well as a friend and the possible challenges you may face on this
journey to sisterhood. It will also help you learn more about the
friends you have around you, their struggles and what they need
from you.

2. Accepting it all starts with you

We'll be diving into personal development. How can we make sure that, by investing in ourselves, we can become better people and better sisters? We'll be talking about everything from emotional to physical and mental wellness, and looking at how to become the best version of yourself.

3. Dealing with your trust issues

We'll be talking about the importance of identifying and healing from trauma and failed relationships, and how these experiences can shape us and our worldview, impact the relationships we have, prevent us from living happy and fulfilled lives – *if we let them.*

4. Being vulnerable and building trust

In this chapter, we're going to share how you can let your guard down and open up to let your friends in. We will also explore the responsibility we have to become sensitive and create safe environments for our friends and sisters.

5. Creating and navigating healthy boundaries

The health of your friendship lies in the boundaries you set. We will talk about how you can let people in but also draw the appropriate lines to help you avoid toxic territories that leave you feeling used, abused and exhausted.

6. Goal-setting and accountability

In this chapter, we'll go into detail about how to set goals and welcome your sisters into your plans so you can journey together and hold yourself responsible with their guidance.

7. Dealing with comparison and competition

By this point, you'll be flourishing and hopefully you'll have found a sister who you can glow and grow with. But sometimes you feel something in your heart that you know you shouldn't. Let's talk about the green-eyed monster – jealousy. How do you navigate comparing yourself to and competing with your sister?

8. Taking a supporting role as a sister

In the penultimate chapter, we'll talk about how to decentre yourself, be self-aware and truly be supportive of someone else's journey, and enjoy doing so.

9. The end of the beginning

This is where we sign off, but it is the start of your journey towards truly thriving in platonic friendships.

● ● ●

Sisterhood is about going beneath the surface both personally and relationally. So, take a deep breath, take your time and know that you're not doing this alone. Do it with a sister or friend so that you can 'grow and glow', as we like to say, together.

CHAPTER 2

What's Your Profile?

What Kind of Friend Are You?

*'Am I actually invested in learning
about you and loving you?'*
COURTNEY

When trying to cultivate healthy friendships, an important question you must ask yourself is *'What kind of friend am I?'* This
question isn't about the quality of friendship you provide (we
have the rest of this book to get into that) but rather the role
you play within your friendships. We each play a unique part in
people's lives. More than just the title we hold as 'friend', 'sister'
or 'daughter', we provide a function and value to those who
choose to journey with us. For example, think about your friends
– who do you go to when you have a dilemma and need some
advice? Who do you go to when you need a good laugh? Who
do you go to when you want to paint the town red after that big
promotion? Or who *won't* you go to when you're in need of help
but you'll always be there to provide help for them? You may
have one go-to person who can provide you with all the things
you need from your friends or you may notice that, based on
each friend's personality and your relationship, you have different
kinds of friends for different kinds of things.

We are all shaped by our unique experiences but we must become self-aware to understand the impact they have on the way we build friendships. They affect how close we allow people to get to us, the help we accept from the people we love and our approach to being a friend. Ultimately, our experiences impact our ability to develop intimacy. So, we've created five friendship profiles which we think help us identify the common approaches to friendships.

1. *The 'open' friend*
2. *The 'demanding' friend*
3. *The 'reserved' friend*
4. *The 'strong' friend*
5. *The 'closed' friend*

This is far from an exhaustive list but these profiles are wide enough to be relatable to most of us. They exist to provide a general guide to help you discover who you are and how you may behave in your friendships. As you read these profiles you may get a 'yep, that's me' moment or think 'that's definitely [insert name here]'. And that's what we want, for you to recognise yourself or your friends in these profiles to gain understanding.

One of the biggest things that can cause any relationship to break down is continual misunderstanding. And we've found that misunderstanding can happen not just from miscommunication but from a lack of knowledge of ourselves. For example, if your friend is struggling to understand why you don't open up to them about your problems, resolving the issue is made even harder when you struggle to express your reasons. So, whilst this may not give you the exact description of who you are right now, our hope is that it provides some language and direction for you. With this, we hope you can gain an understanding of yourself and your behaviours within your friendships, so that you can have necessary conversations with your friends about your needs and desires from them as well as how you can work together to strengthen your relationship.

'But I'm multifaceted, how can I possibly be summed up in one profile?'

Each profile is just a starting point. You may occupy the space of multiple profiles in different relationships. To one person, you may be the 'strong' friend and to another you may be the 'demanding' friend. But it's important to try to identify who you are within each friendship, and who your friends are to you, so that you know what areas to work on within yourself, so you can learn how to cater to your friend's needs.

You've probably heard of *The Five Love Languages* by Gary Chapman, a book which details five ways we can express and receive love to and from other people. You've also probably done one of the many tests and questionnaires online which help you to discover what your love language is. Knowing the way that you receive love – whether it be physical touch, quality time, words of affirmation, acts of service or receiving gifts – can help you outline your expectations in a relationship and enable the people you are in a relationship with meet your needs. We have had many conversations over the years in our friendship about our 'love languages' so that we could be more intentional in making sure we both felt appreciated in the way that we desire. Knowing how you want to be loved, and what you interpret love to be and look like, is a central part of being self-aware. The same goes for knowing what sort of friend you are and understanding the friends you have. If we take the time to know ourselves better, we can love each other better.

We'd advise you, if you haven't already, sis, to read about the five love languages and identify the ways you receive love. Another approach that could help you reflect on your own personal experiences is looking at attachment theory and attachment styles. It's one of our main references for these profiles and we've given a brief description of it below. It's something we often refer to in our podcast episodes.

Attachment Theory

Mainly based on the work of psychologists Mary Ainsworth and John Bowlby, the theory is a framework which aims to explain how our engagement with our primary caregiver in our early childhood affects our cognitive function, mental health and ability to form emotional bonds. They identified three styles of attachment and, in the late 1980s, Main and Solomon added a fourth to the theory, giving us the four attachment styles commonly referred to in the area of social psychology.

Secure Attachment: Characterised by the ability to form strong, secure and loving relationships with others, people with this attachment style are unafraid of intimacy and can trust others. They do not feel panicked when people around them need space away and are better at accepting the shortcomings of other people.

Anxious Attachment: Anxiously attached people tend to be fearful of those they are in relationships with leaving or abandoning them. They tend to be clingy, needy and possessive. They are excessively co-dependent and fear being alone.

Avoidant–Dismissive: People with this attachment style struggle to get close to others and are often emotionally unavailable. They tend to avoid intimacy and sabotage blossoming relationships out of fear of rejection.

Avoidant–Fearful: The characteristics of this attachment style include a blend between the dismissive and anxious profiles described above. Whilst they desperately crave intimate relationships, they avoid them at all cost, often displaying disorganised and inconsistent behaviour.

Knowing whether you have a secure, avoidant, disorganised or anxious attachment style can help you and your friendships by giving insight into your behaviour. With the abundance of literature out there surrounding making romantic relationships work, we can easily be fooled into thinking we only need to learn and know these things about ourselves in terms of our relationships with our partners. But actually, being self-aware and understanding of how your past, childhood and relationship with your primary caregivers impacts the way you relate to every person in your life could be the gateway to success in all forms of relationships that we engage with on a daily basis. So, as you read these friendship profiles, remember they are just a part of the bigger picture of who you are and the key to unlocking the potential of your friendships.

FRIENDSHIP PROFILES

The 'open' friend

The open friend is the quintessential profile many of us aspire towards. They are not only open to making new friends but they give and receive love openly and with ease, often giving people an invitation to build intimacy with them. This allows them to trust and get close to people easily. They typically have a secure attachment style, having been around consistent and responsive caregiving that paid attention to and validated their needs. Thus, they find it easy to model this behaviour to those around them.

They clearly communicate their needs, desires and boundaries and are open to hearing the needs, desires and boundaries of others from a place of security, self-awareness and confidence in themselves and their friendships. They allow their friends to access them on a deeper level according to their displayed actions towards them. In other words, they can discern how much access to themselves and their resources they should give to people depending on their behaviour towards them.

They are also generally at ease with receiving feedback on their actions and character. Whilst it is never comfortable for any of us to hear 'you were wrong' or 'you made me feel bad', the open friend can take in that information and decide for the sake of the relationship or for themselves if and how they will change. They allow the people who they care about to share how they feel and create an environment for those around them to be honest in love.

Don't be fooled by their title – an 'open' friend isn't opening themselves up to receive just any quality of friendship, they have healthy boundaries and standards for those around them which they can confidently express. And whilst maintaining these standards, they give people room to be imperfect, reasonably measuring the effort put forth to meeting the expectations they set. They are happy to give second chances to those they believe will truly continue to try but are not afraid to lose friends who repeatedly miss the mark. They embrace the fact that people come and go, they put in the effort to keep them but expect that effort to be reciprocated.

The 'demanding' friend
The demanding friend is very open to making friends and receiving love openly and with ease, and often communicates their need for it. This allows them to trust and get close to

people very easily, though sometimes, to their own fault, they can allow people to cross their boundaries due to their craving for intimacy. They sometimes neglect assessing other people's character before bringing them close.

It's easy to categorise this as the 'needy friend', and this profile can easily display traits of self-centredness, sometimes putting their needs above others and neglecting the responsibility of reciprocating the intimacy they demand. They may find themselves unintentionally choosing friends who choose to put them first or 'people pleasers', taking advantage of some people's need for validation by using them.

Although they can easily identify and express their needs, they have tunnel vision and often don't recognise the needs of others. Their need for love, attention and friendship can stem from insecurity or fear of being alone, and they typically have an anxious attachment style. They confidently communicate their needs, desires and boundaries but struggle to honour the boundaries of others and can often violate them.

However, as negative as this profile may sound so far, there are a few things a lot of us can learn from this profile type. Whilst the 'demanding' friend can lean towards over-sharing, they know how to be vulnerable, welcoming friends in to build intimacy with them by providing help. This could be why they make friends and good friends so easily; they don't struggle to take off the mask, revealing their true selves and needs, because they never put one on. Many of us struggle to make demands of people – it's a challenge to have expectations of people if you have experienced past disappointment and fear being vulnerable. But this can cause us to struggle to get the depth of friendship we actually desire. The 'demanding' friend knows what they want from their relationships. If they don't receive it, they happily move on and try to find it somewhere else.

The 'reserved' friend

The reserved friendship profile is introverted (this could be their natural temperament or a learned response). This does not mean they are not social or that they're necessarily shy, but they're quite reticent and don't easily put forward their thoughts or feelings. The reserved friend can show up and give you a whole heap of personality but are not so forthcoming with their intimacy because they will not let you close.

They struggle to initiate relationships and are fearful of getting hurt due to past pains or traumas. They have a fear of failed relationships and of being heartbroken or experiencing loss, so they'd rather not take the risk of forming a strong attachment to their friends. This fear can prevent them from fully embracing the love and service of the friends around them, sometimes being scared to let people come close in case the friendship doesn't fully work out or because they struggle with being vulnerable. This person can also stop themselves from being there for other people for the same reasons.

They mostly have a fearful–avoidant attachment style and struggle to communicate their needs and desires, having learned to satisfy these things for themselves from other sources outside of their friendships. They can often do this to try to protect themselves. This profile differs from 'the closed friend', below, because they actually desire to build strong bonds with their friends but are being held back by fear, disappointment, shame or their own hyper-critical thoughts. This profile can also be quite elusive and turbulent in their commitment to friendships, oftentimes becoming withdrawn or distant, not necessarily purposefully.

A great thing about the reserved friend is they have a huge degree of self-awareness surrounding their personal life. However, their self-awareness can easily start leaning towards being hyper-critical of themselves and others because they're operating in the realm of assumption, filling in how they think they are perceived by others with their own self-perception. They can be terrible at communicating their feelings, or may view communicating them as unnecessary, but this ultimately leads to self-sabotage because they actually want to have close relationships. The greatest struggle of the reserved friend is vulnerability and trust.

The 'strong' friend

This profile also has a fearful–avoidant attachment style and struggles with vulnerability. The strong friend knows how to be independent but wants to be interdependent. Their challenge is they constantly find themselves being the pillar for their friends. Their independence is perceived as having it all together – hence this person can often find themselves putting other people's needs before their own because they have a desire to 'fix' things and take on the mantle of 'being there for everyone', while learning to be fine with people not being there for them because it's they who are the 'fixer'. They are the quintessential agony aunt that's always 'fine'.

So, who does the strong friend go to when they feel broken, weak or in need of help? No one. Or themselves. They can lean towards hyper-independence not just because they don't want to welcome people closer, but because they are aware of the struggles they are helping other people face, so they don't want to burden them with their problems. As the one who provides the support for those around them, they can feel like there is an internal and external pressure to maintain an infallible image of strength. That pressure, coupled with their perceived inde-pendence, creates a mask of 'perfection' which they often struggle to take off.

Their suppressed need for intimacy will eventually manifest as some toxic trait. Whilst being a supportive and helpful friend is virtuous, this profile must be careful of becoming proud, arrogant, condescending or rejecting love and affection shown to them. The strong friend faces the danger of viewing their need for love and support as a weakness, believing the lie that if they require the love they give to their friends from their friends, they are no longer worthy of occupying their seat as the 'strong' friend. Therefore, they can also struggle to receive feed-back, which could suggest they are not the 'perfect friend' – as not only can this be a blow to the ego, it could actually cause grief over a loss of their perfect image and extreme guilt.

The strong friend can be very hard on themselves to maintain their ability to always be there for those who need them, often feeling a sense of guilt about having boundaries with their time and emotional capacity. Whilst being very good general communicators, they struggle most to communicate their own needs, desires and boundaries, sometimes because they won't allow themselves to acknowledge them or, as previously mentioned, they just don't think they're important. They are quite similar to the 'demanding friend' in that they struggle with reciproca-tion, just on the other end of the spectrum: they rarely take anything but they give everything. Because of this, this profile typically deals with emotional burnout.

The 'closed' friend

If 'no new friends' was a profile, it would be the closed friendship profile! The 'closed' friend builds a mental and emotional fortress, believing these to be healthy boundaries. They require people to be perfect before 'rewarding' them with intimacy. They can set unrealistic expectations for their friends and tend to project past failed friendships onto current friends without paying attention to the efforts made by the individual friend. Unlike the open friend, closed friends don't allow you to miss the mark with them; they struggle to forgive and have compassion with regards to any failures within the relationship, especially early on in its formation.

They can come across as quite defensive and dismissive, and take pride in their self-sufficiency. They have an avoidant attachment style. You may be wondering how this profile actually makes and keeps friends! They actually, typically, have the oldest and deepest kinds of friendships. They tend to cherish and invest in the friendships they already have because if they have allowed you in, it's because they are sure they can trust you as you've been there for them through the greatest struggles. They hold friendship in great esteem and don't throw the title around loosely, preferring to have very few friends. There is sometimes wisdom in this, but it can be due to general suspicion of the motives and character of other people. They're often the one spotting the red flags and testing people's 'true intentions'.

The closed friend often doesn't communicate their own needs, desires and boundaries. Yet they expect people to identify them, taking offence when they are not met or are violated. In their view, you should understand the needs of friends intuitively. Whilst they believe they are great communicators, they're not. They often act based on their own emotions and conclusions rather than being open to conversation and compromise.

The 'closed' friend closely guards their resources, time, energy and emotional capacity. Those things are reserved for those they deem truly worthy, not because they're trying to be unfair but because they fear being used and exploited by those who are not as independent as them. Because of this, they can sometimes appear cold or dismissive when it comes to intimate relationships and conversations.

Again, whilst this profile may sound resoundingly negative, the closed friend can teach us something about what we as women can so often struggle to contend with – selfishness. You probably just winced at reading that word because we're taught that selfishness is bad, and it's true. Being selfish can stop us from building healthy, reciprocal friendships. However, many of us deny our own needs and desires because we fear being called selfish. We don't consider ourselves and our wellbeing in the decisions that we make or in how much we allow people to take from us out of fear that we will seem 'closed off' and ultimately end up alone, having pushed people away because we resisted meeting everyone else's needs. Whilst the closed friend can take this too far by not allowing anyone close to them because they suspect ill intentions, what we can learn from them is a degree of independence and discernment that stops you falling into the trap of giving everyone in your life the same level of access to you and your resources.

WHO AM I?

Courtney

I used to be the first to put my hand up and say, 'I'm the strong friend.' I was used to hearing, 'Courtney, what should I do? I need your advice,' and happily stepping into that mothering role, providing nurture and guidance for those around me. I used to struggle to ask for help not because I thought I had to keep up appearances (not consciously, anyway) but because I was highly self-sufficient. As the eldest daughter in a West African home, I was often regarded as the second mother to my younger siblings.

Both my parents are nurses and with such a vocation comes long shifts at hospitals and hours committed to studying. Whilst my dad has always been in my life, I was raised in a single-parent household for the majority of my childhood and my mum was my primary caregiver. Born and raised in Ghana, my mum has always had a passion and a skill for taking care of people, so when she got the opportunity, she became a midwife in Kumasi, Ghana. Unfortunately, when she immigrated to the UK in the early 1990s, due to the healthcare system here, none of her qualifications were valid to allow her to practise midwifery. She had to start her medical career again from scratch. After a few years in the UK doing retail and factory work, and other essential jobs such as cleaning, she decided to return to formal education and start the journey to being able to do what she loved again. In 2005, when I was eight years old and my younger sister was four, my mum decided to go back to college and eventually went to university to gain a vocational qualification in nursing.

I really admire my mum's work ethic. She is the hardest-working person I know. Growing up, I saw first-hand just how much she tried and succeeded in providing for us and her entire family. She was burning the candle at every possible end, working on assignments, going to lectures, working long days and night shifts whilst on placement and still had to do a cleaning job in order to take care of her children. My mum's daily routine consisted of waking up at 4am, getting us ready for school (and probably putting rice in the rice cooker for dinner later that day). Then she would take us with her to the GP surgery she used to clean. She'd let us read all the books left for the patients in the waiting room whilst she made the offices spotless, and, after rearranging all the books and magazines my sister and I had flipped through, she'd drive us to our school's breakfast club and make her way to a long day shift on placement from 7am to 8pm, arriving back home every day at 9pm. After making sure my sister and I had eaten, bathed and done our homework, she'd then clean any mess we had made and eat whatever was left over from dinner. Then she'd get to work on university assignments before heading to bed around midnight (only to repeat the same routine the next day).

My mum deserves the world, and a lot of children of immigrants or those who grew up in a low-socio-economic status household can relate to this kind of story. If you didn't, I am sure you can imagine that when your parents are working hard to make ends meet and provide a future for you and those they love, it requires you to step up, mature and learn to take care of the things they can't be present for because of this burden. So, for me, when the bell rang at 3:25pm, I would rush from my secondary school to pick up my sister from primary school or after-school club. We'd get home and, as the older sister and eldest sibling in the house, I would get our dinner ready, help my sister do her homework and get my work done. It wasn't something I resented; it was just something I had to do. I had to support my mother, especially when there wasn't another parent in the house. I became a parent. I know it's something my mother didn't want to happen, as she regularly expresses that it was one of her deepest regrets, having experienced parentification herself as the eldest daughter in a family of six surviving children.

Parentification is the process of a child taking up the role of being a parent to their siblings or their own parents. They take up the emotional, financial or physical responsibility of a parent and it is something a lot of children experience. It leads to the child having to deny their need for attention, provision, guidance, care, affection and attunement from their caregiver. Instead, they learn to give these things to themselves. They learn to be highly self-sufficient, which often impedes them from forming healthy attachments and can later lead to hostility, resentment and struggles with intimacy.

Parentification is a process I wasn't aware of until I did research for one of our most popular podcast episodes on 'eldest daughter syndrome'. In my attempt to find out more to share with our community, I came across a podcast called 'The Place We Find

Ourselves' by Adam Young, a licensed clinical social worker. In an episode titled 'Why Your Family of Origin Impacts Your Life More Than Anything Else' he explains that there are 'two kinds of relational styles that result from being dismissed by your parents or being asked to be a parent rather than a child'. I was triggered to my core after the 31 minutes of that podcast. It was like someone had just described my entire life, poked at the most painful point in my heart and yet had relieved me of so much confusion by putting language to feelings I had harboured for close to 20 years.

After listening to this podcast, doing some soul searching and asking Renée which profile she thought I was, I realised to my complete shock that I was the 'reserved friend'. I would have never considered myself to be an introvert. However, my family and those who get to see me outside of the performance of being the loud, bubbly, funny friend would've said otherwise. Because of my childhood, I had learned not only to subvert my needs from other people but I had become completely self-sufficient in what Adam Young describes as 'affect regulation' –which simply means learning to cope with your stressed-out self by yourself. The way your parents respond to you when you are in a stressed-out state is one of the most important interactions they can have with you. It teaches you about shame, dependence and freedom. When I was a child, I usually didn't have a parent around to attend to me at my most anxious or frustrated after a day of being bullied at school or failing an exam. I had to learn to regulate my stressed-out self alone and carried that behaviour with me into adulthood.

A perfect example of this happened recently when my friends called me up on my lack of communication and participation in certain group activities. I had to be honest and let them know that I was struggling with overwhelm and anxiety because of my workload and personal life. I wasn't necessarily scared to admit it but I was approaching it as an issue I needed to get over on my own. I even considered it quite weak and frustrating that I was dealing with such things. My response wasn't to welcome in support from my friends but rather to retreat into my own bubble, to try to get myself together and solve my problems using my own strength, often causing me to reach emotional, mental and physical burnout. It meant I stopped engaging with my friends and would often miss things like phone calls, messages and events that were important to them, but I hadn't communicated why I had retreated. This left room for them to think maybe their friendship wasn't important to me and I didn't 'need' them, possibly making them feel rejected. This is what made me realise I was more the 'reserved' friend than the strong one because I wasn't there for everyone else's needs, I completely withdrew.

Once I felt like I was more on top of things I would reappear from my little rabbit hole ready to engage in my friendships again. It was sad realising that this made me appear inconsistent, flaky or unreliable as a friend. I couldn't possibly be as present and supportive as my friends needed me to be and it was my lack of communication about that fact that was disrupting the growth of our friendships. I felt a lot of shame and guilt around this and even though I apologised and my friends forgave me, the hypercritical voice in my brain was still telling me that I was a bad friend. Luckily, I am surrounded by some of the most amazing friends in the world who kept expressing and trying to get close to me because they could see past my flaws and appreciated the effort I was making to do better.

This experience taught me a valuable lesson about sisterhood: knowing what sort of friend you are is the starting point to growing into the type of friend you want to be. It's never too late for that growth to take place. You don't have to be perfect before you enter into relationships, you just have to be committed to trying.

• • •

SO, WHAT'S YOUR STARTING POINT?

Maybe you can't relate to being parentified as a child, perhaps you had to become a carer to a family member at some point of your life, or maybe you have struggled with trauma. No matter what it is you've been through, your story matters. You need to think about your experiences and how they have shaped the person, and the friend, you are today.

Activity

This one is simple but it may take you some time.

Thinking honestly about your behaviour and approach to your friendship, try to identify what type of friend you are. We advise that you do this in relation to each close friend you have rather than trying to find who you are across the board because you may function differently in each relationship. Think about the following things to help you assess your profile:

Area of reflection:	My honest answer:
How open are you to being vulnerable and receiving help?	
How often do you provide help and support to your friend by deep-diving into how they truly are?	
Do you feel comfortable and confident expressing your needs and desires. For example, can you and *do you* express how you want to be loved?	
Do you feel like you have to wear a mask or maintain a particular image in front of your friends?	

Once you've thought about these questions and decided what sort of friend you are, do the bold thing and ask your friends which category they think you fall into. Have an honest, judgement-free conversation where they can draw on real-life examples of when you've been that person in your relationship.

Remember this is just to identify your starting point. You are not condemned to being this person forever and you are not incapable of changing just because the past cannot be edited. Your future is still being written by the pen of your present-day choices.

• • •

Start the journey

We can learn a lot from each friendship profile. But ultimately, we should all be working towards a 'secure' attachment style, as embodied by the 'open' friend. Realistically, most of us won't wake up tomorrow having transformed into the perfect friend just because we've been made aware of what it can look like. It's going to take effort, self-awareness and patience. And that patience isn't just something we afford ourselves but also what we need extended to us by those we call friends.

Don't be afraid to be honest with yourself about where you're starting from. Don't be ashamed of what you might discover once you start digging deep into why you are the way you are. You may want to talk these things out in therapy or regularly engage in conversations with your friends about it and that's perfectly fine. You can and should endeavour to explore who you are and how you behave within the context of your community with the help and guidance of that community.

It's important, so we're going to say it again: these friendship profiles aren't fixed, they're starting points. Our friendship profiles can change based on negative or positive experiences in our lives. Don't get complacent but also don't feel hopeless. For example, if a friend takes advantage of your trusting nature and desire to support them you may adopt a more 'closed' approach to friendships, becoming hesitant to share your resources again out of fear. But sisterhood is a positive, transformative force that helps us open up in response to being loved well.

CHAPTER 3

It All Starts with You

How to Become the Best Version of Yourself

'Glowing up sometimes doesn't start with you going up;
you've got to go down.'
RENÉE

Do you know what one of the most fundamental building blocks of the important relationships in our lives is? The scarcest resource we own when it comes to improving the relationships we have with other people? The one thing that, if lost to the outside world, will detrimentally affect others like an exploding bomb? *Ourselves.* This isn't to stroke your ego but to remind you that we have a responsibility to bring the best version of ourselves to the table – not only for our own sake but for the sake of other people. The person you are matters; you matter. The glowing and growing journey isn't just for you to become a 'boss babe' or reach the top of your field (though this is great too!). It's also an opportunity to ensure that you are being the best kind of person for the people you love. You have a profound impact on the people around you. You have the power to make or break them.

You've heard that relationships are about two people sharing responsibility and burdens '50/50' – and you've probably also heard a wise person disagree and say, 'No, they're about both people giving 100 per cent.' This statement is true but when it comes to friendship, we so easily forget it. When we look to make friends, we can easily adopt the 'what's in it for me?' mindset. We look for people whose personalities we enjoy or whose advice we can soak up, or we may simply look for the most popular person. It's certainly not a bad thing to look for people who add joy, wisdom and open doors, but instead of simply approaching your friendships thinking about what you could gain, you also have to ask yourself, what do you give? Honestly speaking, ask yourself, would you like to be your own friend?

OF COURSE I THINK I'M GREAT!

Great, we love that for you, sis, and we truly hope that you are as amazing as you think. A lot of us fall into the bad habit of hyper-focusing on our flaws and we struggle to embrace our strengths and acknowledge our own beauty. But chances are, if you picked up this book then you know that, like us, you're not perfect. And that's great because that level of honesty and self-awareness is pivotal to building authentic sisterhood. We don't want you to highlight or be defined by every mistake that you make; however, we do want you to be aware of them. Some of us struggle to be honest with ourselves about our weaknesses, often remaining oblivious to our own toxic traits and inconsistencies or bad habits because we believe we are justified in having them. And some of us fixate so much on our weaknesses to the point we allow our overwhelmingly negative self perception to hold us back in our friendships. Many of us do both. We are aware of our weaknesses or unproductive habits in some areas in our lives but we are unable to recognise unhelpful tendencies in others. It may be helpful for you to identify your strengths and weaknesses in the various areas of your life where you desire to see success – from your career to your relationships – because one skill you display in one context may be lacking in another.

Touching back on trauma, it can be easy to fall into the trap of believing that because we have experienced pain, we are justified in not being the best we can be towards other people. We can subconsciously believe that because people – including those we've trusted – have dealt with us badly, we don't owe anybody anything. We hear that phrase 'nobody owes you anything' thrown around a lot in popular culture in an attempt to encourage hyper-independence and divest from the collective, but how can you find, build and truly benefit from a healthy sisterhood or community with a lone-wolf mentality? Even the alpha knows that it needs a pack in order to survive. When you participate in sisterhood and you're building authentic friend-ship, you make something of a promise to the people you call friends that you'll constantly try to show up as your best self.

BUT PEOPLE HAVE HURT ME!

Exactly, you were hurt! Think about how much that took from you. The years you spent trying to stop believing the words a bully said to you. Or how hard it was to overcome the insecur-ities that that comment someone left under your Instagram post gave you. Or the many good relationships you missed after somebody abused your trust. As people who have experienced or seen pain, why would we want to inflict it on anyone?

Some of us may be tempted to think, 'Well, people didn't show me much compassion, why should I have to pay it forward?' But doesn't somebody have to choose to stop the cycle and start a new one? As people trying to cultivate healthy, productive patterns in our lives, we have to get to a point where we decide that the change starts with us. Yes, it's a lot easier said than done. And whilst we'd like to think this will be our response to all negative things that happen in our lives, we will be the first to admit that sometimes it's easier to take the less-peaceful route.

BECOMING THE VILLAIN

Villains in films often get given the backstory of having experienced major loss that they feel they need to avenge, or they have a great personal mission which they believe justifies the chaos or evil they inflict. The cinematic devices we're all used to, like the suspenseful music, dark wardrobe, pet cat and random British accent, help us to recognise who the villain is in the movie we're watching. We know that we are meant to hate this character and their questionable morals, and that we're supposed to cheer on our hero-protagonist as they go on to stop their evil schemes, ultimately coming out victorious.

However, we don't have a soundtrack to our real lives, or ominous sound effects that play when someone enters the room. All we have is our intuition and emotions to help us perceive and handle a threat. Both are trained by our natural fight-or-flight responses and cultural/environmental factors, as have been modelled to us through other people's responses to conflict and violence in its various forms. We also don't have the privilege of having our battles with our antagonists and the people who inflict pain on us being confined to a two-hour feature-length film. Many of us face our tormentors every single day because we work with them, go to school with them or call them family.

For a lot of us, unlike the films we watch where the hero reigns victorious because of their unwavering goodness and dedication to taking the moral high ground, we often choose to fight fire with fire – not because we are bad people but because we are defending and protecting ourselves. We build walls that keep people out and learn to make our tongues sharper to show people we're not to be messed around anymore. Or we reclaim some of our power by removing ourselves from the role of the victim and becoming the victimiser, often picking someone who is as vulnerable as we once were to be the subject of our anger.

This becomes our villain origin story. We are both victim and villain. It's the age-old tale of how 'hurt people, hurt people', or those who were once bullied become the bullies. For example, if you were picked on or bullied in school like we both were, you may have found yourself picking on other kids around you in an attempt to exert your own dominance. Because your bully made you feel small, if you could make someone feel smaller, that could boost you up a little bit. This example works in lots of other contexts too – some of us fall into a pattern of gossiping about a colleague because we're insecure about our own performance. Or we teased our siblings to punish them because we felt they were our parents' favourite. Or even when we have that passing thought of 'that person doesn't deserve to have that' because we haven't achieved it yet. Our insecurities are real, our pain is valid, our anger is justified but our response cannot be to make other people collateral damage to our trauma. So yes, you can have a bad day and yes, you can make mistakes, but they don't have to become a pattern. We are the sum of the repeated choices we make – and our choices have consequences.

One thing you'll notice is that villains don't have a lot of friends. As funny and simple as that may sound, bad people generally cannot maintain good relationships unless they act out multiple personas and build their relationships based on deception. If they do have comrades, it's usually fellow villains and bad people. So if you desire to have good friends, you have to step out of your role of being a villain. People with good hearts don't want to be intimate with those who have let their pain and anger consume them. Have you ever heard the saying 'bad company corrupts good morals'? The intimate friendships that you desire with people you consider 'good' won't last long if you don't confront the darkness in you. It probably wasn't your fault that the bright light of your soul was dimmed by the darkness of the world around you. But be encouraged that you *can* go through a process to restore that light and allow it to shine even brighter than before. It's a journey you don't have to go on alone, that journey is your *'glowing and growing'* process.

GLOWING AND GROWING – THE JOURNEY TO BECOMING THE BEST VERSION OF YOURSELF

At the end of every podcast episode, we give our signature catchline – 'keep glowing and growing'. It's a charge to our listeners and the sisters we get to speak to on a weekly basis to keep doing the hard work of evolving into the person they want to be. But what does it really mean, to become the best version of yourself? It's often given as a response to the many questions we have about our personal development journeys. How do I deal with my insecurities? How do I stop comparing myself to other people? How do I find my ideal partner? 'Become the best version of yourself' we're told. It's close to becoming one of those terms that are thrown around so much that they begin to lose its meaning, becoming a bit annoying. When we get used to hearing a phrase a lot, the familiarity means we don't grapple with it because we assume we understand it. But if we really take time to unpack it, it will help us to understand why the 'glowing and growing' process is necessary, as well as why we can get so frustrated on our personal growth journeys.

BECOMING . . .

When you hear the word 'becoming', what do you think of? Maybe you define it as a process of evolution. Evolution is necessary for our survival and it's natural. You probably don't have the same goals, dreams and interests as you did when you were a child. As we get older, we discover more about our values and the expectations society places on us, and our responsibilities only grow bigger. This pushes our mindsets, schedules, habits and priorities to change. This allows us to embrace new things but it also alters our needs and the types of friendships we desire. As we evolve, everything around us must also. Sometimes that looks like losing old friends and finding new ones. But it can also mean having honest conversations with our friends about the transformation that is happening within us and welcoming them on our glowing and growing journey. Having your friends as a support system whilst you're on your path to personal growth is one of the greatest benefits of sisterhood.

We must also be mindful that whilst we are evolving, so are the people around us. It's just like caterpillars going through the process of metamorphosis, breaking forth from their similar-looking cocoons to become butterflies of different size and colours. Understand that as you and your friends go through your own individual journeys of evolution, you're probably not going to all come out looking the same. But you still have a responsibility to support and embrace their evolution. You want your friends to become the best version of themselves. That looks like encouraging them to pursue their dreams and explore their interests, whilst allowing them to navigate life their way.

We can experience feelings of fear and guilt around evolution, especially when it comes to changes in our friendships and relationships. We can be afraid that people will distance themselves from us or that we will no longer share common ground with our friends, causing us to grow apart. For example, if you make the decision to pursue religious faith, you may be scared that no longer participating in certain activities may cause you to lose touch with your friends who still engage in the activities you used to. Or say you choose to continue studying but your friends are in full-time work. You may become a parent whereas your friends might be childless, which may make it a struggle to find time for each other, given your schedules and responsibilities have now changed. These things can be challenging; however, they also provide a great opportunity for your friendship to adapt and for you to be more intentional about finding new common ground. Finding new activities you can do together, inviting them over to your house instead of going out so that you can watch the kids and catch up, or maybe adapting your schedules to make time for each other during the holidays between your academic terms are all examples of workarounds for your new lifestyles.

Be intentional in being vocal about supporting each other. Send your friend simple 'I'm thinking about you' texts, or 'Let me know if there's anything I can do to help' messages. If you can no longer be as spontaneous as you used to be, and/or you can't spend as much time with them because things in your own life have changed, just be honest. You can also put dates in your diary for when you'll go out, specify nights in the week when you'll speak to each other on the phone or note down a time in the year to travel with each other. Even if intimacy doesn't look the same as it used to, it doesn't have to completely disappear from your friendship. You may be changing but your friendships can adapt; they don't have to be thrown away on account of changes in your life.

But sometimes common ground isn't so easy to find. It's healthy and liberating to embrace the truth, that you have different friends for different seasons of your life and seasons eventually come to an end. The end of a friendship doesn't have to be messy or ugly; sometimes it just looks like growing apart, still supporting each other, wanting the best for each other – just from a distance, and that's OK. Sometimes you need to let some space emerge in your friendship so that you both have room to spread your wings. Appreciate the fact that you experienced great things together but it's time to let go so you can embrace the new.

. . . THE BEST . . .

When going on a glowing and growing journey, there is a standard that you must set yourself to meet. A vision you have for the woman you want to become, and expectations that you clearly lay out for yourself to fulfil. This can be in the form of a personal mission statement which details the character attributes you aspire to that will carry you through life. It could be a vision written on a paper which describes the woman you want to be, her accomplishments and capabilities. Or it could simply be a daily to-do list which outlines what you expect to accomplish with your productivity in the day. No matter what it is, you need something which serves as a reference point for what you consider to be your 'best'. Your standard of excellence is unique to you, no one can dictate it to you. It's a subjective, individual and precious image you have for yourself which directs the daily choices you make. But it's important that this is *your* image, as when it comes to becoming the best version of ourselves, many of us embark on a cumbersome journey towards an image of 'perfection' that is projected onto us.

We have romanticised pictures of us waking up at 5am in the morning, getting ready to vibe and meditate before hitting an intense workout, mowing the lawn, saving a cat from a tree and only heaven knows what else may find its way onto our shopping list towards self-betterment. According to research, the global personal development market size is anticipated to reach a staggering USD 56.66 billion by 2027. It's even more pertinent that we talk about this, considering that the majority of self-help consumers are in fact women – at a staggering 70 per cent. So it's pretty clear that the notion of becoming some kind of 'better version' of yourself is something on the radar of many women, so much so that many of us are willing to put our hard-earned coins behind it.

The pressure to become an enhanced woman does not stop there. There's even a name for it – 'Superwoman Syndrome'. Named in 1984, Superwoman Syndrome refers to women who stretch themselves a little bit too thin in their quest to be the 'perfect' woman, often resulting in a negative impact on their mental and physical wellbeing. Women are often plagued with images of this 'perfect' woman. She's the one who works, works out regularly, cooks, cleans, is present for all her children, friends' and partner's needs, is the object of men's desires, the subject of women's attention, pursues her entrepreneurial dreams, volunteers for worthy causes and still has time on the weekend to bake. And she makes it look effortless. It's an unrealistic image many of us feel the pressure to keep up with. And we are sold all types of products, from make-up and skincare to journals and conferences, to help us buy our way to becoming the 'perfect' woman.

Wanting to appear a superwoman is why so many of us fear failure. We become riddled with shame and embarrassment when we say or do the wrong things, burn out or breakdown. This is made worse when it feels like the consequences of our failure are harsher than those for men. We have seen women in the public eye demonised, ostracised and chastised more sternly for their mistakes. Whilst we may have internalised this form of misogyny, it's important for us as friends and as sisters to create environments where women don't feel ashamed for 'failing' to be their best all the time. We must not only encourage each other to dust ourselves off and try again, but we must extend our hands to help our sisters off the ground when they get tempted to stay down under the shame and embarrassment of their own perceived defeat.

In our attempts to reach the standard of excellence we set ourselves and to get better based on our own desires through self-discovery, we are bound to at some point fall short and have to try again. We must take the pressure off ourselves to be perfect the first time round. Imagine you're a basketball player and the first time you practise, you struggle to land the ball in the hoop. You wouldn't let that failure stop you from shooting the ball again when you have a goal in mind to become a better player, maybe even the best. Now imagine that because you're so scared of failure, you start to change the factors involved in you getting the ball in the hoop in an attempt to guarantee you make the shot. The only thing you could really do to guarantee your success would be to lower the height of the hoop to a level you're certain you could make. This is how many of us lower the bar and the standards we set for ourselves. So afraid to fail, we avoid stretching ourselves and thus never reach our fullest potential because we deny ourselves the opportunity to keep trying.

Your 'best' is a level you set yourself to reach. It's ambitious, more than likely requires effort and proves a challenge to your current mindset. You're probably going to, at some point along the journey, fail to accomplish it. That's OK. When you find yourself discouraged by how challenging it is, make sure you are surrounded by friends who remind you of the person you set out to become, why it's worth it and also help you to evaluate why you slipped up and re-strategise your approach to becoming who you set out to be. Allow your friends to help you and hold you accountable.

Accountability

Within sisterhood, accountability is not just about admitting when you've gotten something wrong or when you've failed, it's about keeping you on track. This requires you to be honest about how you are feeling and what you are thinking along the journey, even before the failure happens. Create an environment in your friendship in which you can admit when you are tempted to give up or when you feel discouraged. You'll probably find the support and wisdom you are unable to give yourself in your friends. Give them permission to help you, to tell you when they can see you going off track. Your friends have the ability to see you from a perspective you cannot. They can lend you their knowledge and strength, ultimately helping you become the person you want to be.

It's so tempting to navigate your glowing and growing journey alone because you feel like it is all about you and your personal growth, but it takes a community or a sisterhood to establish and sustain a vision. The voices of your friends can guide the direction you take on this journey; they are a great influence on the future you. Surround yourself with people who are as deter-mined as you are on your mission. Sometimes this can be uncomfortable because it means your friends will have the right to call you out on your blind spots. To tell you when your behaviour is unproductive. Or when your character is out of line with the woman you aspire to become. It can be humbling, but friendship requires humility.

. . . VERSION . . .

Not to get all 'multiverse' on you but many versions of us exist both in our minds and in real life. The 'at work' version of you is probably not the same as the version that your friends see. It is normal for the personality we display to be adapted to our environment. Our desire should be to develop a consistent character which, whilst being adaptive, does not change in essence. This is otherwise known as having integrity and authenticity. You do this by creating a code of conduct you live by, setting a standard for the way you treat people, approach your work and live your life.

There is also the past, present and future version of you – the person you used to be, the person you are and the person you are going to be. On this journey of self-improvement, you must identify the parts of yourself you want to change and strengthen. This will ultimately lead to the person you currently are becoming a past version of yourself – that's evolution. To become the woman you want to be, you must let go of the person you currently are, and that must therefore become the person you used to be.

The challenge with this is two-fold. Firstly, the person we currently are is the one we are used to, and often most comfortable with. This doesn't mean we're happy with them, it's just that they are familiar to us. It's the version of us that doesn't require us to step out of our comfort zone. It's hard to let go of this because as unproductive as the habits we have allowed ourselves to form may be, it feels like an act of compassion to make excuses as to why we might not have met these new standards and expectations. The change we want to see in ourselves can feel disruptive, but as much as you may be comfortable in your current form, if you want to level up, you will have to eventually wave goodbye to the current you.

Secondly, not only have we become comfortable and familiar with the present version of ourselves, so have the people around us. When you decide to become a better version of yourself, it can be difficult for those who have bonded with you to embrace the change. It can be a learning curve to adjust to the new boundaries and standards. Friends need to allow each other to evolve by not holding each other hostage to past decisions and choices which are no longer in line with the person we say we want to be – 'Since when did you start liking that?', 'But this is how you used to do it!', 'This is what you would've done'. It can be very discouraging whilst on your glowing and growing journey to be constantly reminded of your old self and your past, especially as an attempt to hold you prisoner to it.

We must be mindful that there are many reasons why some friends seem resistant to our evolution, and it may not be because of any ill intent. Never assume the intention and heart posture of your friends; give them an opportunity to explain themselves through open and honest, vulnerable conversation.

. . . OF YOURSELF

What do you like? What are you good at? What are you scared of? Who are you? We often ask questions like these of people we're dating but they are questions we also need to ask ourselves. Take time to get to know who you are – and not just as it relates to other people but who you are at your core. If somebody was to ask you, 'who are you?', you'd probably answer by listing the many titles you hold or describing what you do as a job. But who are you outside of your relationships and your output? You are not the sum of the things that you produce; the things you produce are the fruit of who *you* are.

As women, we can become distracted from discovering who we are at our essence. Instead, we divert our attention and efforts towards gaining accomplishments, approval and external validation. None of these are bad but they can easily become a cover-up for our lack of self-awareness. This leads to us pursuing *things* over knowing ourselves. Instead of seeing our roles and responsibilities as opportunities to discover more about who we are at our core (our character, dreams, desires, likes and dislikes), they consume us and become who we are in our totality – thus, we fear being without them because we think that means we will no longer have value or purpose.

Who are you outside of being a mother? Who are you outside of your job role? Who are you outside of your relationship? What are your core beliefs, your personality, your interests, your likes and dislikes? Women are so often told how we should behave, what we should enjoy and what we should stay away from. Instead of trying to conform to the image of the 'perfect' woman that's projected onto us, to become the best version of ourselves is to find the image of the woman we were always meant to be, the one encoded in our unique DNA and personality. We then come to the realisation that that woman is enough. She is the image of beauty we should aspire to. She should be our 'body goals', our 'It Girl' – she's worth being pursued and manifested to the world because there's no one like her. There is no one best version of a woman, only women who are the best version of themselves.

Once we embrace our differences and uniqueness, we unshackle ourselves from the pressure that comes with being held in bondage to an image we cannot ever truly achieve. When we deliver ourselves and the women around us from pressure to satisfy the male gaze and cease to enforce commercialised western ideals of femininity due to our own internalised misogyny, we give each other the freedom to fly and allow ourselves to achieve magical things together.

As clichéd as it sounds, you at your best form is one of the most powerful forces in the world. You have the power to transform lives, shift culture, heal people and change your world. So many of us struggle to believe this but even though you probably are too small to change the whole world on your own, you can change *your* world. You have the power to change the lives and reality of the people in your community, workplace, school and domain when you stop trying to be someone else and truly step into your place, accepting what you are great at, shining in it, strengthening what you are weak at and pursuing what sets your soul on fire. When you walk in that confidence, you become the key that unlocks another woman's freedom. You inspire her to set herself free and live in pursuit of her purpose and unique destiny. And if we really want to change the wider world, it's even more reason for each of us to not only embrace our uniqueness but be unapologetic in sharing it.

We love films, particularly superhero films, and more specifically Marvel films. The Marvel Cinematic Universe has not only provided us with entertainment we have fan-girled over, it has given us with powerful imagery that represents a lot of the dynamics we experience in our interpersonal relationships.

The Avengers are a team of 'Earth's mightiest heroes', coming together to defeat all manners of evils which launch themselves against Earth, freedom and justice. But imagine if a time of battle came and the Avengers wanted to enlist the help of Thor to fly across galaxies and realms, but the God of Thunder hadn't lived up to the claims of Norse mythology because he had spent his whole life trying to become as big, scary and green as the Incredible Hulk? Something he could never be, not only because he hadn't had the same exposure and experiences, but also because he was made to be someone else.

There is so much injustice happening all over the world, especially for women. Alone, each of us may not be able to change much but together we could change the world. If we all put our effort towards reaching our own potential, we could collaborate to build great things, establish legacies and break down walls that have held us back.

LET'S BUILD A COMMUNITY, SHALL WE?

Courtney
I initially had the idea to create a sisterhood community in 2016 during my first year of university. I didn't know whether it should take the form of an on-campus society where women could meet up, a series of events across different universities or an online forum where women could chat and share advice and stories. Like most of us with a lot of ideas, I just let it fall to the back of my brain and focused on other things I was working on at that time.

I thought about it a few times in the years following and, even though it was a good idea, I never really knew how to truly build the vision of a sisterhood community. I didn't even really know what that meant. I started a series on my YouTube channel called 'Letters To

My Sisters' but it didn't last for very long. Despite this, it was one of those ideas I just couldn't shrug off.

Then, one summer's day in 2018, a few weeks after graduation, Renée and I were in Nando's and I don't remember how the conversation got there, but I told her about the idea. As usual, she was supportive and told me to just start it, and that she'd be happy to help in any way. A year later, I had the idea to turn 'Letters to My Sisters' into a podcast and just call it 'To My Sisters', which I would host on my own. I thought about bringing on my female friends to have conversations with about their stories and their journeys.

In autumn 2019, I invited Renée to come to my office where we shot the first episode, titled 'Frenemies'. We talked about friendship and how we had been able to support each other through the different phases of our lives. She had just graduated from Harvard and I was one year into building my company, so I wanted to explore themes such as how to be a supportive friend, dealing with comparison and how to avoid jealousy. We recorded the episode but I had absolutely no idea what I was doing with the equipment so you could barely hear us on the audio recording – we sounded like two people whispering in a big room.

Because I was discouraged by how bad the first episode was and I was building my own company already, I just let the idea of starting the podcast go. Then the pandemic hit and we did an Instagram Live together, as so many people were at the time. After that, I had a 'eureka' moment. I called Renée and told her we should start a podcast. We thought of a name for weeks and I realised maybe this was what 'To My Sisters' was meant to be. Maybe it was a vision I was meant to share with Renée – not only in telling her about it, but building it with her.

The rest is history, really. This book you're reading, the community we're building and the impact we have is something I never could've done alone. Not because I'm not skilled but because it took the combination of mine and Renée's unique abilities to make it happen.

Many people often ask us what it's like being best friends and business partners. Some see it as a recipe for disaster and I understand why. But the truth is, alongside loving and liking each other, Renée and I respect each other. We respect the intelligence and talents each of us possesses. We believe in each other's competence and decision making enough to let the other person take the lead on certain things. This would be so much harder to do if we had not taken the time to embrace our own individuality and become secure in it. If we hadn't set a standard of excellence which we hold ourselves accountable for upholding. And if we hadn't given each other permission to hold the other accountable to our dreams.

• • •

WHAT'S YOUR DREAM?
ACTIVITY

Have you ever heard the phrase: *imagine the woman you want to be and show up every day as her?* This activity will help you record your thoughts about the woman you want to be so you can set this as the standard you try to live up to. This is not about the woman you think you *should* be, it's about the one you desire to grow into. Dream big and try to break through your limiting beliefs. This isn't about what you think you deserve or what you're confident you could make happen – it's about what you want. We'll think about the technicalities later. If you feel like you don't know what that is, that's no problem, you can come back to this exercise later.

Before you get to writing, close your eyes (after you finish reading this chapter, of course!) and begin to visualise who you would like to be this time next year, or in five years or even ten years. If you struggle to see something for yourself, you can draw inspiration from a woman who inspires you, so long as you realise this can only serve as the starting point; you will still have to create a vision for yourself, which you'll be able to do the more you discover your unique talents, purpose and values. Here are some things you might want to take notice of when you imagine the best version of yourself:

- What does she look like?
- What does she do?
- Where does she live?
- What has she accomplished?
- What is she good at?
- How does she make the people around her feel?
- How does she feel?

You may see this as 'daydreaming' and therefore a waste of time but it's one of the most powerful things you can do. Everything you see around you started as just a thought, a vision in someone's mind's eye before it became a manifested reality or object. If you can see it with your eyes closed you know it can exist.

In each of the outer circles on the next page, write down what you see for her in the different areas of her life. You can choose the life areas that are important to you, in which you want to see the most change and growth. Write the names of these areas on the line at the top of each circle. For example, you could write: health, career, personal finance, relationships and education. Below the heading, in each of the outer circles, write a description of what you see for yourself in these areas. Describe the goals and vision in each area of your life.

In the middle circle, write down who you are at your core. This could be your values, attitude, outlook on life, the philosophies and principles you believe shape the world or the virtues you aspire to possess.

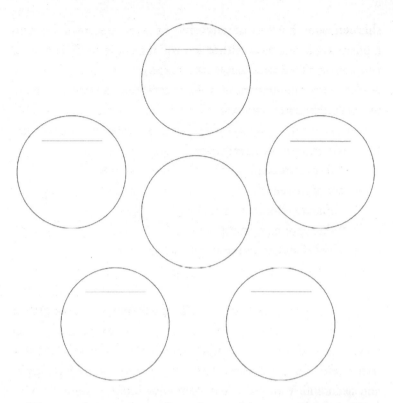

Next, make a separate list of everything you feel is holding you back right now from becoming that woman you want to be. This could be an insecurity you're battling, or a lack confidence or some resource. Just be honest and comprehensive about what you think is stopping you, holding you back or proving to be an obstacle.

Then write down one thing you're going to do this week to combat one of the things listed above. Just one! Trying to change everything about our lives all at once will only lead to overwhelm and anxiety, so give yourself grace and set yourself up for success by taking it one step at a time.

So, for example, your 'one thing' may be to read a chosen article published within your desired career field so that you can sharpen your knowledge and skill, if your dream of holding a position of influence in that industry is being held back by a fear you don't know enough.

Your only challenge this week is to complete that one task. Once you feel like you've mastered that, plan a new task for yourself that's in alignment with tackling something else holding you back or, more generally, that you know will help bring you closer towards becoming the best version of yourself.

So, the steps are:
1. This is what I want . . .
2. This is what's stopping me . . .
3. This is what I'm going to do about it . . .

SHARING AND CARING

Once you've recorded your vision of your best self, talk about it to a friend you trust. Let them know what you're trying to do and accomplish. You don't have to give them a complete plan but use this as an opportunity to invite them on the journey with you by letting them support you and hold you accountable. Take time to then listen to their dreams, what are they trying to build and accomplish in their life. How can you support and encourage them to get closer to becoming the best version of themselves? This is an activity you can do with your friends regularly when you meet up and speak to each other.

As simple as this activity is, it's a recipe for success. Write down a vision, take repeated small and do-able practical steps, make sure you have accountability and make it a reality.

• • •

USE WHAT YOU HAVE

A lot of what you need to become who you want to be is already in you. The rest of it lies in the community around you. Surround yourself with people who are committed to unlocking your poten-tial and enjoying the process of doing so with you. Become someone who also invests their time, effort and resources into unlocking the potential of others. The people you have around you matter; they can be the difference between keeping your vision alive and seeing it grow and mature, or watching it and your passion for it slowly die because of the lifeless words you hear.

BUT I'M TIRED OF CONSTANTLY WORKING ON MYSELF

Then hit pause. You may be feeling slightly overwhelmed by all the information out there on how to become better. You may be growing weary from constantly being pushed and it could have led to you asking *when will it be enough?* There will always be room to grow and change in our lives, new areas of ourselves to explore and behaviour to reflect on because we never know everything about ourselves. Whilst continual reflection is good, you're also free to take a break to just be. This doesn't have to be a defined period of your life during which you decide you're no longer going to grow – that would be impossible. Growth and adaptation are a sign that you're alive. However, you can confine your intentional self-development to specific times in your day or your week to stop yourself from hyper-focusing on your mistakes. You may have more intense periods of working on yourself, but you should never let your self-development journey become unproductive by filling you with dread, fear or self-loathing when it should give you hope and insight.

Your glowing and growing journey isn't about adding one more 'self-help' book to your Amazon cart or buying yet another journal. It may not even be a matter of starting from scratch, but rather picking up where you fell off. Put to use the resources and knowledge you already have rather than thinking you have to keep trying new methods to approach problems. Stop overloading yourself with information, sis, and start putting some action into your goals. We'll be diving more into the practicality of goal-setting and habit changing in chapter seven. But for now, remember this: you can and are allowed to change.

BUT THIS IS JUST THE WAY I AM, IT'S THE WAY I'VE ALWAYS BEEN

It's never too late to change if that's what you desire. Every day presents a new opportunity to turn your life around, to rebrand, to evolve into something new or to choose to invest in a different part of yourself. It may be hard but that doesn't mean it's impossible. Allow yourself to explore the possibility of becoming your dreams, hopes and desires manifested.

CHAPTER 4

You Don't Understand,
I Got Trust Issues

Overcoming Trauma and Failed Relationships

*'Entering into healthier environments and
relationships with people, really magnifies the
dysfunction you once tolerated as normal.'*
RENÉE

It is impossible to go through life without experiencing some kind of pain. It might be physical – falling off your bike the first time you take it out for a ride. It might be psychological, like dealing with a mean comment or two under the picture you post on social media. It might be something you consider a 'surface' trauma – a comment made by an uncle or aunty at a party about your weight. Or it might be a deeper trauma, such as unspeakable physical abuse at the hands of someone you know and love. Despite the best efforts of those who care for us, whether our parents or others, it seems that trauma seeps into our very psyche and becomes a part of the fabric of our lives and identities. It's a fundamental part of the human experience that seems inevitable, and one we cannot escape, though we try our best to.

That sounds neat, sis. A little poetic even. So, what's that got to do with me and my sisters?

It has everything to do with you and the sisters. Absolutely everything. You see, our lives are essentially an accumulation of our experiences up until a certain point. Everything you currently are is a sum of everything you've ever lived. There are a number of very well-known studies which delve deeply into how the experiences we have at key developmental stages during our early childhood and adolescence impact on how we process emotions and our behavioural profiles in adulthood. Taking it a step further, we even carry the deep pains of our ancestors across space and time. In the seminal book *It Didn't Start with You*, Mark Wolynn demonstrates how the traumas of our parents, grandparents and relatives can live on in our unexplained and reflexive responses to trauma – depression, anxiety, phobias, personality traits. Things we just *do* with no hesitation in the presence of very specific stimuli. *It Didn't Start with You* was such a groundbreaking book as it really unpacked the reality of holding onto multiple variants of trauma – some of which were inflicted before we were even born. Known as secondary PTSD, some of us are dealing with symptoms and consequences as a result of things that happened way back in the past. As much as we are individuals with our own agency and choices, a lot of the way we think, feel and engage is a direct result of everything we've been through.

When we think about healing as women, we often filter it through our preparation to be an ideal spouse or mother figure. *Heal for the next generation*, we're taught. *Become whole*, so that your partner doesn't have to spend your life together trying to mend a broken vase, gluing together the cracks that keep appearing. The implication is that you must be healthy enough to form the centrepiece of the imaginary family you're expected to have at some blurry, undefined point in the future. But why do we never apply the same logic to our friendships? Why do we neglect to look at the ways in which our experience of trauma can actively impact the way we create and maintain relationships with our sisters? Why does the way we relate to the people around us, right now, always fall by the wayside? Perhaps we can chalk it down to the social norm of understating platonic and non-romantic relationships but becoming healed and whole is necessary in the quest to have fulfilling female relationships.

Trauma can be pretty ugly. If there's one thing that we're both super upfront and straight up about, it's this fact. *Trauma is ugly.* No one wants to talk about it, not *really.* No one wants to deal with it, not *willingly.* No one wants to admit that they have it, not *quite.* Admitting that you are dealing with trauma can be uncomfortable because it almost feels like you are admitting to being tainted, broken or hurt. No one likes admitting that they were placed in a vulnerable position, and that they've been hurt before. But it's one of those things that simply has to be done. If you don't do it, chances are everything in your life will suffer – from your own mental health to the people that you care about most.

Healthy relationships require pruning. They require commitment, accountability and a willingness to examine yourself in order to do better and be better. You can't show up for anybody – not even yourself – if you're still knee-deep in trauma you're unwilling to face. You may not believe us but it's true. Our own experiences of trauma have impacted the progression of our friendship at many different times. That's because it actively changes and dictates who you are as a person, if you let it.

YOU DON'T KNOW MY STORY

The classic response.

According to the American Psychological Association, trauma can refer to either a 'distressing event, or our psychological/

emotional response to such an event'. Trauma can occur at any age and cause harm that lasts long after the immediate experience. Trauma can be recurring and it may trigger both short-term or long-term responses – mentally, physically and/or emotionally. Traumatic experiences can leave you feeling frightened, threatened, rejected, neglected, abandoned, humiliated, unsafe, powerless and so much more. You can experience trauma as a result of your social identity, from your friends, family, community or even environment. Trauma can sometimes directly cause mental health problems. Some mental health conditions, like post-traumatic stress disorder (PTSD) or high-functioning depression, can develop as a result of experiencing trauma. Lots of other unhealthy psychological coping mechanisms may develop as a result of traumatic experiences. From eating disorders to exacerbated narcissistic tendencies – trauma can be one of the biggest contributing factors to why we are the way that we are.

Self-sabotage is one of the most common responses to traumatic experiences. We've all been there, sis. It's one of the greatest defence mechanisms we employ. You know the feeling? When it feels like things are going a little too good and you start to clam up and look for the exit plan before the house falls down? Or you start to pick apart holes in your life that aren't actually there, but you're pretty sure will exist in t-minus two weeks? Yeah, that's what we're talking about. The anxiety and panic you feel constricting your throat aren't a figment of your imagination or a weight that you have to carry alone. In fact, it's a very common and normal feeling that many sisters can resonate with. Unfortunately, normal doesn't always mean healthy.

Many of us self-sabotage in our own lives and our relationships because of the trauma we've experienced in the past. We've developed low self-esteem and have internalised the belief that we do not deserve to have good things in our lives. Past negative episodes might have convinced us that because we are unworthy, it is better to cut short or ruin our relationships early, so that we don't have to feel greater pain later down the line. Or we self-sabotage because we seek to control our situations. Since we believe that our pain is inevitable, it may seem like the only way we can feel in control is to be the very thing that caused us so much pain in the past. The victim becomes the perpetrator in a sad, unending cycle. The worst thing about self-sabotage that not only do we end up sabotaging ourselves, we end up sabotaging other people in the process of trying to protect ourselves.

Self-sabotage can manifest itself not only in the way we engage with others but in the way we engage with and see ourselves. We might overindulge in some vice – food, sex, alcohol, exercise, self-deprecation, drugs, social media, or whatever addictive substance or activity – in order to blunt the negative emotions that we have yet to deal with. This type of self-sabotage is hedonistic and destructive, as it destroys the basis of any healthy relationship you could've had with anyone else, by destroying yourself.

Yet another common response to trauma is complete and utter shutdown. Cue 'I got trust issues' as a broken record. The fortress begins construction and the walls go up, shutting you off from the world around you, hiding your emotions. It seems like the phrase 'I got trust issues' is something we've internalised, memorised and *glamourised* despite it being the sad reality of many broken sisters. Stonewalling is when you close up shop and make it extremely difficult for anyone around you to feel as though they can get close to you. You might be known to your friends as the icy, calm and collected one. Perhaps you're the 'blunt' one, the one who 'says it like it is' because you've ascended to a place where it is no longer possible to hurt you (or so you tell yourself). You've built your ivory tower and you intend to stay there. But in reality, you know that the reason you built it is because you have been broken before.

Can you relate? You've been hurt so many times, or betrayed so deeply, that the next contender interested in trying to love you has to go through an obstacle course just to get through the front door. And that's just the front door. Woe betide the worthy contenders who get through to the next level. There are so many checks and balances that many quit before the quest is done – which allows you to convince yourself that they were weak and unworthy. Could it just be that the walls you put up are too high? That the landmines you set to destroy the threat simultaneously blew up every chance at real friendship you ever had?

POKING THE BEAR

Renée

I'll be the first to admit that both of the examples I'm about to share were me. To a great degree, they still are, though I'm working on it. In my own personal life, I've experienced a lot of trauma. I've experienced the realities of extreme poverty, the aching pain of sexual assault, the agony of handling a broken home. It's often difficult for me to express these things aloud, or even acknowledge that they were things that happened to me, because I thought that my acknowledgement of my trauma meant my trauma had won. That, in order to keep some semblance of control over myself and my identity, I would have to bury these realities deep inside myself, never to be revealed, so that I could forget they ever happened. Perhaps if I forgot these things, then that was that – they never happened. But they did, and they were gnawing away at me every day. They would manifest in a facial expression, an involuntary reaction, a withdrawn response. They would flash across my mind in an instant, then remain there for many hours afterwards. I thought the way to be free of my trauma was to completely detach myself and yet what I hadn't realised was how much it was causing me to detach myself from my relationships.

It was a couple of years into my friendship with Courtney when I really found enough courage to talk about these things. I had never been to therapy (although I'm presently going) and I had never told a soul about what had happened to me. No one ever asked. I had become comfortable with characterising myself as the 'strong' friend in my friendships. You know, the one that everyone goes to for advice or to share their woes with. I always feared and dreaded the day someone would be brave enough to ask me. To poke the bear and force me to come out with my story, making me face the experiences I had buried so deeply within the confines of my psyche. Push me to hold up the broken glass splinters I had swept under the carpet. Fortunately, Courtney was one of those few people in my life that I could trust. She was one of the only ones willing to go the distance. She was the first person who was brave enough to poke the bear.

We were having dinner together at one of our favourite restaurants. I reckon it was Nando's – one of those restaurants that is neither poor nor spectacular but hits the spot. I remember the weather was slightly cloudy outside – downcast, as though rain was imminent. It was right after an event we had been invited to, relatively close to our homes. The conversation had halted a little, as it naturally does when we tuck into the meat and bones of our peri-peri chicken. And then suddenly, Courtney looked at me, cocked her head to one side, and said, 'Renée. I actually don't know so much about your personal life like that. I've shared so much of mine. What's good?'

I think I might have shed a tear. I could've bawled, but I was far too used to playing my role as ice queen for that. I might have chosen to keep it all in, brush it all away. But Courtney, in being so open and honest about her own experiences, her own trauma, had inadvertently given me permission to bring all my dirty laundry to the *table. With a shaky voice, I told her. I told her about some of the parts of myself I had never said aloud. I told her about the time I wept for hours and hours after the first time my sexual assault experience happened, and how I blamed myself for putting myself in that position in the first place. About the times I had planned to disappear when I reached the lows of my eating disorder, and sometimes ate half a meal a day, if that. I told her about the times I had considered ending it all, when the pain was far too much to bear. I told her a lot. More than I had ever told anyone. More than I had ever told myself.*

She listened patiently, every so often furrowing her brow or reaching out to rub my arm. I don't know what I was expecting from her – but it was in those moments I realised something. Trauma can just as easily build closeness in your closest friendships as it can rifts.

• • •

We tend to think of our experiences of trauma as reasons to close ourselves off to other people. No one needs to know our deepest, darkest secrets. The dirty laundry. The mess under the bed. The ice or fallen food we kick under the fridge in the hope that we don't have to deal with it. Perhaps we tell ourselves that our trauma isn't really a big deal in the first place. So, this kind of sort of very massive occurrence happened during a critical juncture in your developmental trajectory. So, what? Surely it's not that big a deal? You don't have to disclose something that's not actually an issue? Or sometimes we even tell ourselves that no one can really understand our trauma, not seeing that with each mental and emotional stretch of distance we put between ourselves and our pain, the further and further away we get from those that could love us better than we could ever imagine.

Many of us are out here perpetuating our own trauma. In trying to protect ourselves, we lock away any capacity for sharing or acknowledging our pain, with the result that we close off any opportunity to acknowledge, heal and overcome it. We shut the door to any opportunity for our friends to see us at the apex of our brokenness, despite that often being just what the doctor ordered as part of our healing process.

I CAN DO THIS ALL ON MY OWN

Trust issues syndrome and 'doing it all alone' is killing the sisters. The belief that we were meant to experience and deal with traumatic episodes in our lives alone is preventing many of us from moving on in a substantive and meaningful way. You cannot carry this load by yourself. Believing that you can is what will eventually put the final nails in your coffin. Burdens are made to be shared and there is no shame in sharing. The narrative of being an independent, self-sufficient woman will only take you so far, and using this caricature to bury the deep pain you feel in the centre of your chest cannot continue. You don't give power to your problems or your abusers by talking about them. In fact, all the power resides with you. It's only when you are brave enough to make these experiences even more real in speaking them aloud, in sharing the reality of their impact on your life, that you can employ the help of a sister to break down the impenetrable fortress you put up in your mind.

Now, that's not to say you should be ready to spill your deepest, darkest secrets to the next gal pal you meet over brunch. Mind you, we're sure that avocado toast and bottomless mimosas are a great conduit for opening up your soul! What we are trying to say is that this isn't the only way to start these kinds of conversations. This is more a gentle flag to help you understand that, firstly, you have some unresolved trauma leaking into your life and, secondly, you need to focus on cultivating friendships and communities that will aid your healing process in a healthy, reciprocated manner. Rome wasn't built in a day and neither are enduring friendships that are conducive to sharing your life experiences. You need to start building intentional safe spaces into your life – that is, if you haven't already.

Now, at this point, we know there are sisters reading this who don't have any friendships, or have very few friendships, that fit the bill of 'long-lasting', 'enduring' or 'comfortable'. Perhaps you think no one really knows you, or you've been hurt so many times before you've stopped actively investing in the kind of deep friendship we are talking about here. If that's you, sis, here's the reminder you need: you were never meant to travel through this life alone. We know you've been hurt. We know you've had your heart broken. We know you might be using this as a defence mechanism to help protect yourself and the last ones who may be standing in your close circle. It isn't healthy. It certainly isn't right, either. The burden just grows bigger and bigger, and the distance between yourself and the people around you only increases. Don't let these feelings fester without uprooting them and working on rebuilding intimate relationships.

Some sisters might feel as though they just attract bad luck. You've had so many negative experiences, bad encounters and genuinely awful people enter your life, you may think it's not even worth trying again. Whether you've been unlucky in romance or in friendships, it just feels as though no one has really chosen to stick around with good intentions. You may have had people trample all over the boundaries you erected, so that you felt violated when they took all you had to give, and left you high and dry. There may have also been people who abused your trust or contributed to your low self-esteem and self-worth. Perhaps you have been in emotionally or physically abusive relationships, or even experienced this in your early childhood. This may have left an impression on your mind that you don't deserve good things or good people. Perhaps, as you read this chapter, this is the first time you've read this about yourself – you deserve good things and good people in your life.

Yet another issue many of us contend with is the expectation that the people around us will know how to deal with our trauma. That the people who are meant to be in our lives have mind-reading capabilities or an intuition akin to a sixth sense. The kind of person that just 'gets it', you know? Unfortunately, that's usually not the case. Oftentimes, we need to be more forthcoming with building, investing and sharing. Whilst love might be a feeling or an emotion, its expression must be active and learnt over time. People do not simply love us – they must learn to show us love in a way that we can receive it, and vice-versa. Such a great feat requires a great amount of vulnerability. Each time we open ourselves up, sure, we potentially might end up getting hurt. But there's also the possibility to experience deep love, acceptance and help, like you may never have known before.

Start slowly.

If you already have friends that love you deeply, or a few people around you that you trust, start those conversations. Now, your friends are by no means therapists. However, sometimes it's not simply professional assistance we need. Sometimes, you just need community. Sometimes, you just need a good friend. Sometimes, you just need a sister. Get used to articulating your pain and leaning on the strength of the people around you.

If you don't have people around you that you feel comfortable enough to confide in, then you need to do some work on developing those relationships. These take time, and honest reflection as to why you find it difficult to make these connections. As much as you have been hurt by previous experiences in friendships before, if it has happened on a recurring basis, you must confront the common denominator – you. How have you also fallen short of your potential in developing these deep relationships? What have you done that facilitated repeated friendship break-ups or how have you attracted people to your life that ought not to be in it?

DON'T FORGET – RECIPROCATION IS KEY

Some of these sentiments might not resonate with you. Perhaps sharing comes more easily to you and you've always been able to open yourself up to the people around you, or you've always had the necessary vocabulary to articulate the things that have caused you great pain in the past. Or perhaps you are lucky enough to have a go-to sister-friend for the deep, heart-to-heart surgery that is often required in life. If that's the case, it's great that you have a sister to lean on. It's an honour and a blessing to know that you're already benefiting from having someone who is invested in your growth and happiness. However, it begets other important questions.

When was the last time you listened to *their* open wounds? How have you showed up for them in their darkest moments? When was the last time you were a shoulder for them to cry on? Much like the *demanding* friendship profile, you might be used to all the support without also providing support. The key word here is *reciprocation*. Many of us think of ourselves as the guarded, Miss Independent type of gal we described above. However, it's perfectly possible to either occupy space on the other side of the spectrum or actually be both types of friends to different people. You might be shut off to the whole world and most of your friends but have a few choice sistren who you feel you can *really* talk to on a level. This is why it is important to evaluate the bulk of your friendships. Whilst you may be thriving and healthy in one, you could easily be the toxic counterpart in another.

When you examine your interactions with your friends, would you say that the fair share of load is 50–50 overall? Of course, relationships aren't always exactly equal. We aren't playing tennis and sometimes your friend has to do 80–90 per cent of the work, and other times you do. That's just the way the cookie crumbles; the reality of life is that sometimes, one friend will have to carry the other through a particularly tough time. But have you ever taken up that role? Or have you merely used your friend as a free-for-all support vending machine?

How many times have you used your friend instead of a counselling service? Unless your friend is qualified (and in most cases, we're prepared to bet they aren't) you've been unleashing the fall-out from your trauma without actively cultivating a recip-rocal, comfortable environment. You may have been oversharing your trauma to the point of actually closing off opportunities for your friend to share. You may have set up your friend to be the 'strong' friend, when they could just as easily be as close to falling apart as you are. The only difference is they, unlike you, do not have someone to share their woes with.

What if I'm the problem? What if it's me? Here, it gets ugly. It's always awkward to acknowledge your shortcomings. One of the things we most encourage our sisters to cultivate is self-awareness. Self-awareness is all about opening your eyes to your responses, behaviours and personality traits. The thing about self-awareness? You need to be cognisant of the bad as well as the good. And sometimes the bad is *really bad*. What if you aren't just perpetu-ating or enacting a trauma response? What if you were the first villain in the story? The top of the food chain? What if you were a childhood bully, or verbally, emotionally or physically abusive to friends and family? Is there grace for you too?

DOING THE WORK

You may have been hurt in your past friendships or relation-ships, to the point where you're starting to think you'd be better off alone. You've probably also had moments where you've been so abusive, negligent, mean, rude or dismissive to your friends, that you wondered if it's possible to change your ways. Or, maybe you've experienced both at different times in your life. That's normal too. You aren't beyond saving and you too deserve fruitful friendships. You just need to be willing to *do the work*. Really take some time thinking about your character and evaluate the way you've been treated by, or treated, your friends over the last few years. Are there any alarming patterns there that exist outside of your friendship? Have you allowed your trauma to turn you into the strong friend – or to turn you into the friend that takes, takes and takes until there's nothing left? Have you been a victim? Have you been a villain? Or have you been both?

We're willing to bet that you've been both. After all, human beings aren't perfect. In fact, we're pretty much known for being a flawed bunch of creatures. We mess up time and time again, even as we strive and aspire towards being better. And that's OK. Acknowledging the reality of that duality will set you free, as well as give you an ample amount of grace to give to those around you. We fail at things, and often. It just so happens that failing at relationships can hurt us in ways that we often do not imagine before we feel the ill effects. This is irrespective of what role we have played. Whether you've been a victim or a villain, a failed relationship can hit like a truck – even if you were anticipating its breakdown.

It's important to use our experiences as learning oppor-tunities – either to show us how we can be better or how we can enact boundaries to allow others to treat us better. They needn't manifest in negative trauma responses. This isn't to invalidate your response but rather to empower you and arm you with the knowledge that you needn't be held captive by them. You can choose to initiate a healing process that will do wonders for your current and future relationships. You can decide that, today, the next version of you will acknowledge your experiences and start the necessary work of overcoming. You can decide not to be a perpetrator and instead be the full stop at the end of what could otherwise easily turn into an ongoing cycle. The cycle can break with you. If you've come to the realisation that you need to unveil your trauma, and reciprocate that vulnerability, here's how to do it *practically*. These following exercises are intended to be completed as part of the journey towards wholeness and becoming a better sister.

OVERCOMING TRAUMA
ACTIVITY

This activity can be completed alone but to make the most out of it, we encourage you to write down the answers to these questions and share them with a friend you feel comfortable enough to do so with.

1. Be honest with yourself
The first step to overcoming trauma is being honest with yourself about your feelings and your experiences as a friend. To this end, you must ask yourself some key questions. Where are you falling short? What things are you good and bad at, in terms of how you relate to your friends?

ACTION: Write down your top three strengths and your top three weaknesses. If you are doing this with a friend, swap a piece of paper and ask them to write down your three strengths and three weaknesses. Do the same for them and swap back your papers to compare. When finished, try to identify at least one thing you will both do differently, to address one of your stated weaknesses, in the next week.

2. Recognise your trauma and your healing stage

Recognising your trauma and the healing stage you are currently at can help you to be practical in your means of tackling your current feelings. Here are the healing stages we follow:

Stage I: I have not acknowledged my trauma consciously.

Stage II: I have started to acknowledge some of my trauma.

Stage III: I have started to acknowledge my trauma and I have started working on healing from it.

Stage IV: I have partially healed from my trauma.

Stage V: I have fully healed from my trauma.

ACTION: Identify up to three traumas you have experienced and note down the various stages you believe you are at in your healing process next to them. If you are doing this with a friend, in addition to writing down your top three traumas and stages, discuss the ways in which you can move up a level in your trauma for each one you have named.

Identifying and sitting with the traumas you have experienced is important to your healing process. Many of us find it difficult to deal with trauma as we haven't found an effective way to articulate our experiences or the feelings and reactions that have arisen in response to them. In fact, many of us are unsure as to how deeply these run. Being practical and methodical will help you gauge what kind of help you need and prompt you to develop the vocabulary to articulate this to someone else. By doing this, you will be able to figure out whether this is best shared with a friend, a therapist, or both.

We'd recommend you do the first two tasks on the same sheet of paper, with at least one or more friends. Once you've noted everything down, swap your full paper with your friend (if you are doing this in a group, swap around so that no one has their original paper) and discuss each point. For the second action point, read aloud each other's traumas (if comfortable to do so) and discuss what you've learned about your friend as a result. How has the knowledge of their experience changed the way that you perceive them? How has this changed the way you perceive your friendship? How can you be a better support system and friend to them?

3. Co-create environments of vulnerability

Most issues in this world can be solved through basic, honest conversations. But it's the simple things in life that can be the most difficult when put into practice. We may know intellectually that communication is key, yet many of us actually lack the capacity to hold conducive conversations without stonewalling, blowing up, negatively processing our emotions or thinking too much about the other person involved. Successfully and truthfully communicating things we find difficult is very much underpinned by the existence of a safe space – one where you feel comfortable enough to share, transparently, what you think, feel and are going through. Environments of vulnerability can take time to foster and are created by investing in friendships, spending more time learning about each other and genuinely being supportive in times of trouble.

Be intentional about being vulnerable with your friends, bit by bit. Perhaps it'll be over some food in a restaurant. Or maybe at a friend's house or on a walk. When it is that the moment comes for you does not matter – what matters is that when it does come, you don't run away from the prospect of opening up. Embrace it.

ACTION: Note down one thing you'd like to do with your friends that involves conversation. This could be a walk, a dinner or even a picnic. Once you've had the opportunity to discuss, agree on the most popular conversational activity and set a date in the next two weeks to execute it.

• • •

FINDING RESOLUTION

Dealing with trauma is hard, but necessary. It is never the responsibility of your friends or sisters to completely help you resolve your issues. It's more a team effort but you're very much the captain here. You can only be helped if you want to be helped. You can only heal if you choose to start the healing process. You can only overcome if you desire to overcome. We know you've gone through a lot, sis. This life is filled with a multitude of pain and torment, but the seasons of stormy weather should never cloud the entirety of your life's journey. They should never define the way you engage and relate to other people. You might be a product of your past but your past is not all there is to you, and it does not have to determine your future.

For the sake of yourself, your future family, your sisters – choose to take the awkward, uncomfortable steps of committing to overcoming your trauma. Break the cycle, become the woman, build the relationships.

One step at a time.

CHAPTER 5

Please Don't Judge Me

On Vulnerability and Building Trust

*'Just because you've gotten accustomed to carrying the
load, doesn't mean you should be carrying it alone.'*
COURTNEY

According to the Merriam Webster dictionary, the definition of
'vulnerable' is 'capable of being physically or emotionally
wounded' or 'open to attack or damage'. The word itself sounds
scary, so it's no surprise that many of us fear it. But it is our
resistance to confronting our greatest fears that holds us back
from experiencing the greatest of loves.

Many of us are scared of being vulnerable because it makes
us look weak and opens us up to judgement. We're afraid that
if we express things like being hurt, are honest about our failures
or admit to struggling with anything, that we will be viewed as
helpless, 'a mess' and weak – labels many of us dread being put
on us. We dare not confess with our mouths what we fear in
our hearts – that we are an imposter, not good enough, unde-
serving of the love that is shown to us and not as strong as
people think we are. But if we do not open the door to our heart
for the people we trust to see our humanity, how can we welcome
them in to help us, know us and truly love us? How can they

know the fullness of who we are if we hide the parts of us we believe are too ugly to see? How can one possibly build intimacy with a person they never allow close enough to know all of who they are? If you want to build authentic friendships, you must bring every part of yourself to the table. Even the parts you believe you should hide.

Conversations around vulnerability have recently done great work in reframing our beliefs and comfort with the word, teaching us that vulnerability is a strength. Rather than being 'open to attack or damage', it's the ability to be emotionally intelligent enough to identify what we are feeling, as negative as those emotions may be, and expressing those feelings and thoughts to other people. That level of emotional exposure and openness isn't easy to reach and it shows that a person has commendably won the internal battle against shame.

Many of us have feelings of shame, embarrassment and humiliation when we think about aspects of who we are, our past and our experiences. They are emotions which lead to us closing ourselves off and holding ourselves back because we do not want to experience them again. Many of us may have been vulnerable, transparent or honest at some point and experienced someone vocalising their disapproval of us, leading to a physiological and emotional response. Think of that heavy feeling in your stomach, the lump in your throat, your cheeks turning red and rising in temperature, your heart racing or the tears that well up in your eyes when you feel like you've just done or said something 'wrong'. Our body's response to shame and embarrassment is to tell us that we are scared, so we kick into our fight or flight response. And, of course, not only does our body have a reaction to this perceived threat, so does our heart. We make a decision within ourselves to never open ourselves up to such judgement or pain again. We tell ourselves that to be vulnerable is dangerous. So, when we decide to embrace being vulnerable in any relationship it is a display of strength, because we are facing danger head on.

The description of vulnerability as a strength is very helpful for us as human beings because it is our survival instinct to present ourselves as strong. However, we as women must be careful to not create a toxic relationship with the word 'weakness'. We must resist harmful tropes of being the independent woman who doesn't need anyone, 'the strong Black woman' or the 'perfect' mother. Please allow yourself to say you're hurting. You're allowed to crack under pressure and be sore from burdens. It doesn't make you any less of the amazing, evolving woman you are. Open up and admit 'I'm tired'; sisterhood is where you can find rest, safety and help.

Whilst we can tell ourselves that embracing our weaknesses is a strength, we should not use that statement to cover up the fact that, when it comes to some parts of our lives, we are in fact weak. It is normal for us to feel fear, doubt and to fail. The truth is women, like all human beings, go through struggles with mental health, insecurity, addiction and so much more. We are not superhuman – and even if we were, superheroes still have their kryptonite. When we approach vulnerability as just a display of strength and not an embrace of weakness, it can lead us to think that our struggles can only be discussed once we have conquered them. So we find ourselves being honest on the other side of our battles, when we feel we've 'got ourselves together', rather than when we are in the middle of our mess. We get it, all of us are different. Some of us prefer to deal with parts of our personal battles alone rather than with other people, and whilst we do think it's better done within community, sometimes it take a while for us to get to the point of welcoming others into our mess. In your early stages of healing you may retreat into some moments of solitude to contend with your personal battle but you should not isolate yourself during this entire journey especially not due to feeling shame. It is this fear and shame which stops us from experiencing the freedom and safety sisterhood provides.

At To My Sisters, we always say that healing is a journey. It can be long and ugly. A way that many of us display our internalised pressure to be perfect is by wanting to show up in our relationships having arrived at the point of having 'fully healed', as though that were measurable, quantifiable and a destination rather than a process. We only share our stories when we have slain our Goliaths, re-emerging from having retreated within ourselves with the giant's head in hand, with shouts of victory and encouragement for the people around us. We dare not let people see us in the part of the story that produced the testimony. We won't allow an audience to view us break a sweat as we draw back the slingshot like David, struggling under the pressure of the challenge. Because if they saw as much as a drop of perspiration on our forehead, or a shiver of nervousness, they would realise that we felt fear, that we were unsure if we could truly defeat our tormentors. That we were not perfect warriors, that, in fact, at times we doubted our own strength. We're sure the 'strong' and 'reserved' friends out there can relate. Being strong can become such a huge part of your identity and some of us become so reliant on it that you begin to believe that to admit weakness, or even feel 'weak', would be letting yourself and those around you down. It would be a hammer to the porcelain mask of perfection you wear to cover up the truth that you too feel fear, pain and doubt.

WAIT, YOU WATCH PORN TOO?

Courtney

In April 2020, I made a YouTube video titled 'I Was Addicted to Porn for 10 Years'. It was at the beginning of the nationwide 'stay-at-home' mandate in the UK as a response to the emergence of Covid-19 as a global pandemic. Articles and reports were being published about the rise of loneliness and internet pornography consumption – and I knew the two were related. Human beings need interaction and intimacy; if we are denied it, we will do everything we can to simulate it. As someone who had made transparency a mission for their content, I started to feel compelled to share my story around pornography with my digital community. It's probably the video I have had the most fear about and been most scared to create.

I knew it was taboo, and an awkward subject. It was something I had never discussed with my friends and family in depth and yet here I was about to put all my business out on the internet. As much as I knew it would help people, a huge part of me didn't want to do it because I was worried that it would destroy people's perception of me. 'Women don't struggle with porn, that's a guy thing' was one of the biggest lies I had told myself., I felt embarrassed to admit even to the people I loved that I had indulged in watching it and that at a point in my life, it was all I wanted to watch – so much so that it was no longer a want, it had become a 'need', which I felt I was unable to say no to. But I made the video nonetheless, hoping that anyone currently trying to stop watching porn could find some encouragement as they faced their own battles of trying to stop watching it because they didn't want to do it anymore.

Like I said, for many of my friends and family this was the first time they were hearing about it. You can imagine how scared I was when my mum called me into her room a few days after the video was published. She welcomed me to sit at the foot of her bed as she lay down, scrolling through her phone, and then proceeded to say in Twi, her mother tongue, 'So, Akos . . .' (one of my traditional Ashanti names) '. . . what is pornography?'. My younger sister had run into the room at this point, presumably to see how this would play out and diffuse the situation if need be. We both looked at each other and burst out laughing.

The conversation my mum and I had afterwards was completely unexpected. I thought she'd be upset that I had put my story out there – she is far more private and reserved than I am – but instead she let me know that she was proud of me for sharing something that I thought would help people. She also told me to be wise, as this level of exposure would bring different things and people to me. I don't think she knew in that moment how much I needed to hear her words of support and wisdom. I was already battling shame, which I hoped would be swallowed by the greater sense of purpose I had within me. The fact she made this into an opportunity for me to open up more and have a conversation with her about my struggles, turned what could have been a moment of conflict into a chance for us to draw closer and become more intimate.

During the weeks that followed, I got many phone calls, texts and DMs from people commending me, confessing to me, and seeking help and companionship as they privately struggled with the same thing I had. The numbers that I had come across in my research showed that internet porn was a growing industry and issue amongst millennials, Gen Zs and women. But what actually hurt me most during these conversations was the fact that a lot of the women I knew had felt like they struggled with their relationship with porn in the past had experienced the same feelings of shame I did, and had gone on a journey of battling that ALONE, because they were too afraid of the judgement that they thought would come with being honest, transparent and vulnerable.

I wasn't upset at them, I understood them perfectly. I was only too aware of the societal taboos surrounding women and sex, which impede us from being honest and vocal about being sexual beings. I was frustrated and angry for us! Each of us had had to navigate our sexuality, as complicated and scary as that area of self-discovery is, on our own. We hadn't had access to the wisdom and support of the other women in our lives who had themselves privately already done that work. I thought of all the time, sleep and joy we had lost because we were riddled with so much shame, which could have been avoided if we had been vulnerable with each other. If we had just rendered shame powerless by confessing to the people we love and trust we could have gone on the journey of fighting our battles together and it wouldn't have been as tiring and heavy. We could have shared that burden; the stories and wisdom we would have received from other women could have been the head start most of us needed towards freedom. I felt like shame had robbed us of true sisterhood.

My video had broken the initial awkwardness and the conversations I got to have with the women in my life because of that immediately made us feel closer and more comfortable with each other. I realised that our vulnerable conversations were an opportunity and a tool to build intimacy. Being vulnerable, honest and open about our experiences, fears, shortfalls and struggles allowed us to take our friendships from familiarity and engagement with what we each presented on the surface, to an acceptance of that which is inside of us. Sisterhood is about forming connections with our sisters that run deep. So, whilst it is easier said than done, we must confront and overcome our own feelings of shame if we want true sisterhood to flourish.

• • •

A lot of us carry around so much condemnation and unfor-
giveness for ourselves. We feel immense guilt surrounding some
of the things we have done and that have happened to us.
Letting go of shame is a huge part of healing from trauma,
and whilst it's difficult, it's necessary if we want to truly become
our best selves and experience freedom. Some of us struggle
with shame because when we go through something traumatic,
negative, embarrassing experiences can breed a feeling of infe-
riority and foster excessive self-criticism. We think that the
people around us who we hold in high esteem wouldn't have
made such a mistake or found themselves in such a position.
They wouldn't have allowed themselves to get to this point,
they would've done better. But the truth is we are all more
alike than we think.

Think of it this way. From time to time, you may let your house
get a little bit messy. And whilst you're used to your organised
mess, if somebody was to come over, you'd probably spend a
few hours cleaning and tidying in preparation for their arrival
because you wouldn't want them to judge you, and you know
they may form a perception of you based on how you live. So,
after throwing things in closets and cupboards, you welcome
them into a spotless house which almost looks unlived in.
Your visitor compliments you on your home and forms the
perception of 'wow, she's really clean' not knowing that it
looked quite different a few hours prior. You probably did
all this because you knew – or at least you believed – that
your guest's house was also spotless and clean. That they
would never neglect their household chores like you do sometimes. But the truth is, people's homes are probably just
as 'messy' as yours (bar the people who live at either end

of the clinically sanitised or grossly filthy cleanliness spec-trum!). It's usually the knowledge that someone is coming over that gets the majority of us into deep cleaning mode. If no one's expected, the laundry often sits in unfolded piles for a few days before it's put away and we let the pots and pans linger in the sink 'soaking' whilst we binge watch our favourite Netflix series. It's normal! It just feels like something we should all hide because every time we're invited to someone's house, we're presented with a spotless sanctuary. Are you seeing the cycle? And how this same story plays out in other areas of our lives?

Everyone has a 'backstage' – a place of preparation that looks and feels chaotic and that you don't show to the world and most of the people you engage with on a daily basis. The problem with living in a 'highlights reel', or being part of the 'announce-ment generation', is we are hyper-exposed to people's front-facing, put-together images and stories, rarely getting to see the process that goes into making it happen. It can lead to many of us falling into the trap of 'keeping up appearances'. This isn't just about 'keeping up with the Joneses', or the Kardashians, because in comparing ourselves to other people, many of us are more like Hyacinth Bucket in the old British sitcom *Keeping Up Appearances*, feeling the pressure to maintain the images we create around ourselves. This mindset, which inevitably leads to shame about our shortcomings, is often inherited. Like wealth, property and language, shame can be passed down from generation to gener-ation.

Phrases like 'don't air your dirty laundry' or 'what happens in this house, stays in this house' can create toxic environ-ments and lead to people not asking for much-needed help, even to get out of threatening situations, all in the name of keeping up appearances. We may not have been explicitly taught about transparency, honesty and vulnerability when we were growing up, but behaviour around them will have been modelled to us as we observed other people's handling of private matters. Doing the work of embracing vulnerability and confronting our response to shame and embarrassment is necessary in ending the cycle of dysfunctional behaviours and unproductive or destructive patterns which can continue down the generations.

Some of the abuse, violence and poverty some of us have experienced or witnessed has been generational. It happened to our mothers, aunties, grandmothers, great-grandmothers and so on. These generational traumas become generational secrets because of shame. So afraid to ask for help because they feared being judged or punished, the women in our ancestry may have understandably hid the realities of their struggles from the people they loved and the girls they gave birth to. But that shame hindered a cross-generational sisterhood and the passing down of stories and experiences which could have become inheritable wisdom.

Our hope is that the sisterhood revolution births a generation of women who break that cycle. Nothing and nobody are to blame here but shame. It has silenced the cries of many women and robbed their mothers, sisters and friends of the intimate opportunity to wipe their tears from their faces. How much of our mothers' souls have we not discovered because of the unspoken rules which govern our respective cultures?

Intergenerational sisterhood is important. Whilst we sharpen the friendships and relationships we have with our peers, we must also place value on our vertical sisterhoods with the women who are older or younger than us, who assume the roles of mentors, friends and family. Many of us can relate to having strained relationships with our mothers or older female figures in our lives, perhaps even those we work with. It sometimes feels like they force standards on us without grace, and it can breed anger, resentment and conflict. We must make a unified effort to confront these feelings, both in order to not replicate them and to facilitate our healing and trust in lifelong female friendships.

ROLLING IN THE DEEP

Being vulnerable and transparent doesn't mean you have to bare your soul to the whole world! You must set and honour your own personal boundaries and maintain whatever degree of privacy you need, while ensuring the people you allow yourself to be vulnerable with have proven themselves trustworthy. If vulnerability cultivates depth in our relationships, we must be wise in discerning who we get into the deep with.

Think of your life like the ocean. At the beach, we see loads of people enjoying the water by simply dipping their toes in. It's casual and doesn't demand much awareness. But when you look out, as the water gets deeper, there are fewer people. We know that the further we swim out into the ocean, the more craft, commitment and care we need to take in our swimming and navigation. Not everybody can handle being in the deep; it requires maturity, sensibility and an acceptance that anything could be out there. There is more to discover, more to wade through. There will be very few people who prove themselves qualified to become familiar with the deepest parts of your soul. You may only have one or two friends like this in your life – those are your sisters. And whilst they are few and far between, it is necessary to find them, as you don't want to be stranded in the deep alone. That's how you drown.

The first step you must take if you are going to invite your friends to build a deeper, more meaningful relationship with you is to confront and come to terms with the parts of yourself and your story which you have hidden deep. Take off the mask in the mirror first. Confront the truth of what lies behind the tough exterior and put-together image you present at work, online or to your family. If you're struggling with that, find people in your life and online who have taken off their mask and be inspired by their dedication to presenting their true and authentic selves to the world.

CREATING A SAFE SPACE

First of all, you're not being vulnerable with 'people', you're revealing the most sensitive parts of yourself to your *friends*. That title means something. These are people who you love and who care for you, and therefore, they are people you have chosen to believe in the best for you and of you. We live in a world where all you have to do is turn on the evening news or listen to a true crime story for you to lose your faith in people's humanity. People can be wicked, mean and unpredictable. But the people we choose to call our friends should be people we believe to be 'good', whatever you consider that to mean. If you don't trust that your friends want to keep you safe, respect your privacy and not hurt you, then are they really your friends or just people whose company you enjoy? If you believe they are more attached to the idea of who you are and what you offer them than you believe they are there for you at your essence, then what you have is a clique and not sisters.

Unfortunately, the clichéd portrayals of female friendship in sitcoms and reality TV shows have not only caused us to question the possibility of solidarity amongst women, they have made us doubt women's trustworthiness. Scenes of women gossiping, backbiting and using their private confessions as public entertainment has coached us to play our cards close to our chest. When we gossip about each other and the things we have revealed in confidence, we violate each other's trust. It's a red flag that says, 'this isn't a safe space'. We must do all we can to ensure that our sisterhoods and friendships are spaces where we can feel safe to be vulnerable. A place where, when we open ourselves up, we won't be attacked, damaged and wounded, but instead handled with care and honour.

Creating a space of safety is paramount in building authentic friendships. We often don't think about it but we must ask ourselves whether we truly feel safe with our friends and if we have created environments where our friends feel safe with us. Another of the red flags which scream, 'you're not safe here!' is being judgemental. Being judgemental and holding someone accountable are two different things and we must learn the difference if we want to be helpful and not destructive to our friends. After managing to overcome the shame and embarrassment that gatekeeps our vulnerability, the last thing we need is the other women in our lives judging, blaming or harshly chastising us, privately or even publicly, for our mistakes. The truth doesn't have to be administered harshly in order for it to be honest and helpful. Accountability and growth happen best in an environment of care, tenderness and empathy.

It's also very important that we never forget that vulnerability is a two-way experience; it requires a response and we must be mindful of the way we respond to people's openness, lest we cause them to never want to open up again by reinforcing their feelings of shame.

Vulnerability cannot be forced. All we can do is create an intimate environment and be patient enough to wait for the other person to open up. You can create that environment by giving what you hope to get back. Your decision to be vulnerable gives your friends permission to open up to you. In her book *Daring Greatly*, Brené Brown dives deep into the power of vulnerability and our struggles with it. She explains that many of us desire for the people we are in relationships with to be vulnerable with us, but we refuse to be vulnerable with them because we adopt the viewpoint that 'vulnerability is courage' in them and 'inadequacy' in us. We cannot be attracted to vulnerability in others and yet be repulsed by our own. It is this kind of hypocrisy that hinders people from opening up to us.

No matter our instinctive response to what is revealed to us in moments of transparency, we must maintain the principle of being empathetic and sensitive. Even if we disagree with or disapprove of what we hear, we must at the very least honour our close friends and the sisterhoods we have built by not gossiping about them, spreading their secrets or speaking of the intimate things that have been revealed to us, apart from to others whom they trust enough that they have also chosen to tell – unless absolutely necessary for their own safety and/or the safety of those around them.

Another key to gaining the confidence of your friends is to be consistent. You must build a track record of integrity by treating all your friends with dignity and respect. A sister is someone who is mindful of you and fights your corner when you're both in and out of the room, so it's important for us to remain consistent in the way we speak of our friends when they're not around. Think about how hard it is to trust someone who doesn't necessarily talk about you but gossips about others they call 'friends' to you. Surely such a person is capable of doing the same to you when you're not around? We show people whether we are trustworthy by demonstrating how we handle and cherish the trust other people have put in us.

A different way you can nurture trust in addition to this is being intentional about creating experiences and memories with your friends. As simple as it sounds, a way to create intimacy is simply to make time for your friends. It's not enough to just let your friend know you're there for them; you must make your presence felt and show them they are worthy of your time. Show up when you say you will and to the things that matter to them. Spend quality time building rapport. We can be deceived into thinking that commenting under an Instagram picture or liking a LinkedIn update post is enough to let people know we're checking in on them. That works for para-social relationships and acquaintances, but if you're going to build relationships of depth you need to close the distance and go the extra mile, putting in effort worthy of the closeness you desire to see. It takes a considerable time and energy commitment but a core element of sisterhood is the cycle of expenditure and replenishment. Our friends are both the cup we pour into and the well we get to drink from.

LEARN TO LISTEN

Becoming confident in the way we express ourselves is a core part of our glowing and growing journeys. However, when it comes to building any relationship, we must train ourselves to master the other half of communication – listening. The ability to listen is so powerful because not only does it help us to learn more about the person who's speaking, it also signals to them that they are worth listening to. It gives them confidence to continue to share and not shut themselves down because they think their voice, thoughts and story are unimportant.

If you feel as though your friend doesn't create enough space for you to be honest, seen and heard, sit them down and tell them just that. They may naturally be a louder, stronger character than you but it doesn't make you less important or deserving of having this relationship meet your needs. They probably aren't taking up all this space because they're trying to take it away from you, so give them the opportunity to create space on the stage for you.

On the other hand, if your friend lets you know that they haven't felt like they can be vulnerable and honest with you, accept that feedback as an opportunity to build a stronger friendship by responding with effort. We won't always get everything right within our friendships and that's OK. We must create an environment where we can give and receive feedback without passing judgement. Judgements are final, they suggest that we cannot change, whereas feedback is an invitation extended because we are hopeful for change. Listen to both the constructive criticism and the praise you receive about the friendship you give. Whilst the former isn't always comfortable to hear, it is necessary if we want to become better to the people we love.

Listening requires us to decentre ourselves. Whilst many of us may go through life with 'main character syndrome', a core element of sisterhood and building solidarity is knowing when to get off the stage and pass the mic – we'll dive deeper into this in chapter nine. Understanding when your role changes from being the one who is sharing and leading to the one who is listening and supporting, because you must make room for your friends to be themselves and show themselves. It is in learning how and when to step out of the spotlight that we make space to hear other people's lived experiences by giving them the room to tell their stories, perspective and needs, moving from allyship and solidarity through to sisterhood.

As you listen, you must hear the needs behind the words. You may just be required as a listening ear, or you may need to be solution-oriented, or you might have to think about how you can make your friend feel happier. Sometimes we can struggle to articulate what it is we need in a given moment from the people close to us. Sisterhood affords us a degree of intimacy which at times means our friends know what we need without us needing to explain it. There is a degree of 'knowing' that comes as a result of the intimacy that vulnerability births.

VULNERABILITY AND THE FRIENDSHIP PROFILES

We can all battle with shame but some of us have a better relationship with being vulnerable. Here are some of the ways the different friendship profiles often relate to vulnerability. It is worth returning to these, not only for you to reflect on your own friendship profile and how vulnerability may work for you, but to help your interactions with the women in your life.

The 'open' friend
The open friend does not fear being abandoned by those they're in relationships with, thus they find it easier to be vulnerable and transparent as they are secure in their attachments, meaning they are confident that the people in their life will stick around

after they see their shortcomings. They demonstrate this too in their response to the vulnerability of others, as they are forgiving of failure, aware that people are flawed and fallible but still hopeful that they can change.

The 'demanding' friend

The demanding friend can be self-centred in their approach to vulnerability. They can often be emotionally overexposed and lack discernment when deciding who to let cross their boundaries and see or influence them in their most sensitive times. Despite being aware and patient with their own shortcomings, they can be unforgiving of other people's, often holding them to a higher standard.

The 'reserved' friend

The reserved friend will present the best of themselves in fear their vulnerability could push people away. They do not believe that everyone can handle seeing their true depth and so would rather explore it alone. They may fluctuate between pushing people away and allowing them to get close depending on their own feelings about their issues. Their inconsistent behaviour may make them seem untrustworthy at times.

The 'strong' friend

They can easily fall into the trap of being judgemental and often struggle to be vulnerable because they are dealing with perfectionism. They can also feel immense feelings of shame and guilt and may put in more effort to hide these things or make sure their perceived 'imperfections' go under the radar. But they will often be the one present and chosen by their friends as support in their times of vulnerability, as they work hard to prove themselves to be trustworthy.

The 'closed' friend

They will rarely if ever allow themselves to be vulnerable for fear of letting people get too close. Because they avoid and dismiss intimacy, they will not reveal their vulnerability easily, even if the people around them have proven themselves trust-worthy. Whilst they themselves may be trustworthy, they rarely put in the effort to be present as other people attempt to be vulnerable with them.

THOUGH WE ARE HURTING, WE HAVE HOPE

There is no room for pride and ego in friendship. Vulnerability requires us to display humility. It is humbling to inspect ourselves and discover we are fighting feelings of guilt, shame and embarrassment. It takes humility to then show our imper-fections to the people we trust. But as much as it may seem scary, there is something so reassuring about knowing that whilst someone is aware of your imperfections, not only do they still love you, but they hold you in the highest esteem, enough to trust you. Someone who sees your intrinsic value and the beauty of your soul despite everything good and bad that you've been through and everything commendable or unfavourable you've done.

This kind of love borders on unconditional and is transform-ative. It is a love that requires effort and work, but also grace and patience. We have to be in this for the long haul and commit to each other as we venture into the deep. This means not becoming complacent under our titles as friends or sisters. We cannot assume that because we hold these positions in someone's life, we are owed lifetime access to the deepest, most intimate parts of their soul. Trust is earned and maintained; we must prove ourselves worthy of it through our character and actions, by ensuring our sisters feel safe in our company and friendship.

We may think that to be 'radical' in our solidarity to each other means to do and be more. But sometimes radically pursuing love, sisterhood and freedom is to simply present all of who we already are, no more or no less. Maybe the most radical thing you can do in your life is to be authentically you. A person's true beauty is only seen when they are authentic. Think about why it is the authentic and original pieces of art that are always the most valuable. Even when artwork is 'flawed' and time hasn't treated it well, it can still be restored with special effort and care. So even if all you have to reveal right now is a broken heart, a weary soul crushed by shame or a struggling mind, share it with a sister.

Like we see in the centuries-old Japanese art form of *kintsugi*, broken pottery can be put back together again; sisterhood is the gold that turns our broken vessels into a more beautiful masterpiece.

CHAPTER 6

Let's Draw the Line Here

Creating and Maintaining Healthy Boundaries

'Boundaries are the way in which we communicate
to ourselves that we are worth respecting.'
RENÉE

One of the greatest challenges we face in our relationships is determining precisely how much we are willing to let people in. Who will be allowed to uncover the 'real' us? The good, the bad and the very ugly? How far can we open up the worlds that reside on the inside, with the hope that whoever we entrust with the stars of our internal universe will know how to keep them shining – and not, instead, create a black hole? Opening up is always challenging because it requires transparency and vulnerability. It also requires the understanding that everyone around you is human and that as flawed human beings, we are bound to fall short in some capacity. How do we create and maintain healthy boundaries which acknowledge all of these complex factors?

Popular culture in the twenty-first century has glamourised our tendencies to shut off, close down the walls and build an impenetrable fortress that does not even entertain the thought of allowing another breathing organism to cause you harm. Many of us are self-caring ourselves to loneliness and solitude. In reality, good relationships are about negotiating the lines we continue to draw in the sand and breaking down some of these intangible walls we have created. It is about creating bridges and sharing the various parts of yourself with people who are willing to co-labour with you during the journey we call life.

Broaching the subject of boundaries is something women tend to have great capacity for when it comes to our romantic relationships. Social narratives around femininity, feminine energy, motherhood and becoming a spouse make it easy to conjure up imaginary rules to abide by pre, during and post the 'dating' phase. From girlhood to our late womanhood, we are taught to declare boundaries to prove ourselves to be the fairest maiden of them all. But what of the boundaries we set for ourselves – and, just as importantly, the boundaries we create for our fellow sisters? How do we begin to conceive of implementing boundaries in the realm of friendship?

Boundaries are a 'real or imagined line that marks the edge or limit of something'. So, in essence, boundaries describe our ultimate limit. What are the things, actions or words that signify that we have reached our point of no return? Boundaries operate in a vast array of settings – the platonic, familial, romantic and professional – as well as many other spheres. When it comes to building healthy female friendships and connections, boundaries enable the creation of a comfortable, healthy and mutually beneficial relationship and a greater sense of shared sisterhood.

BOUNDARIES: THE NITTY-GRITTY DETAILS

Boundaries – where do we even begin? The perennial question. How about we start with understanding what boundaries are and how they exist in our lives? There are a variety of different types, so here are a few that you may either already have, or may consider implementing:

- Physical boundaries: Physical boundaries are all about your body and physical space – the tangible bits. This can include your personal space, your privacy and basic material needs like food, sustenance and shelter.
- Emotional boundaries: These boundaries are all about your feelings and emotions. Your emotional boundaries concern the decisions you make around your capacity to be vulnerable and transparent, as well as sharing personal information or experiences which may have had profound emotional repercussions on your health and wellbeing.
- Intellectual boundaries: Intellectual boundaries concern thoughts, ideas, beliefs and politics. These boundaries may be manifest in your choice to discuss specific topics at a given time, or you may decide the parameters of when, within a relationship, you feel comfortable sharing these parts of yourself with another person.
- Time boundaries: Time boundaries are pretty straightforward – they concern how you choose to spend your time, in accordance with the priorities you have articulated for yourself.
- Material boundaries: Similar to physical boundaries, although more concerning your actual possessions. Material boundaries are about what you choose to do with what you own, such as your money and other goods.

Not only are there different types of boundaries, there are specific characteristics of boundaries that can help you under-stand how you currently set, or may want to enact, your boundaries. In various psychological circles, the three major characteristics of boundaries are known as rigid, porous and healthy boundaries.

- Rigid boundaries: If you are the kind of person who has rigid boundaries, you're definitely highly defensive and probably a big stonewaller. You shy away from being vulnerable and don't tend to have many close relationships. You may present as strong, or unusually blunt, though most people don't know that much about you. And woe betide them if they try! You are quick to put people in their place, and that place is always several hundred metres away from you. Sounds a lot like the avoidant-attachment style we discussed earlier on in the book!
- Porous boundaries: If you have porous boundaries, chances are you're comfortable with oversharing and are on the people-pleasing spectrum. In fact, you may be people-pleasing to the detriment of your and their health and welfare. You find that people tip-toe, edge or fully trample over boundaries that you may or may not have voiced to them . . . again, and again, and again.
- Healthy boundaries: If you have healthy boundaries, you most likely have reasonable boundaries that can be negotiated depending on the context and need. You know how to say no and how to stand up for yourself in the event of being violated, and, whilst you aren't a people-pleaser, you do take the time to build mutually beneficial relationships that are respectful and reciprocal.

In reality, few people fit so neatly into one category. Many of us are all over the shop. You may have a few friendships with healthy boundaries, and then there's that one friendship where you just can't help but overshare. Or you have that one friend who, when you think about it, you're just a teeny tiny bit afraid of pushing for more information on particular parts of their life . . .

THE REALITY OF IMPLEMENTING BOUNDARIES

OK girl. *Seriously.* Nobody is perfect and believing you're a total failure isn't going to help you get the shining vision of the ideal friendships you've crafted in your head. Firstly, let's do away with the perfect image. Whilst we encourage you to vision cast and set your standards and boundaries in your life, clinging to an idealised image of what relationship boundaries should look like can actually do more harm to these relationships than good. If you're expecting the people in your life to ALWAYS get it right, we have some news for you. They probably won't. Even the people that have known us the longest, or love us the most, get it wrong a few times. It's important to extend a hand of grace – especially since we aren't always capable of living up to our own boundaries, values and principles. The most important things to remember when it comes to boundaries are clarity, consistency, and effort – not perfection. Whilst we strive towards healthy boundaries, we won't allow ourselves to be consumed by the fallacy of perfect boundaries. For example, you might have started getting super-strict about the time you give towards your friends on a given day. A one-hour catch up. Nothing more, nothing less. As perfect as those 60 minutes may be in your head, it also may be completely thwarted by the knowledge of a new breakup – now your friend *needs* ten more minutes of your time to work through some of her emotions and experiences. It might be a little bit distasteful and insensitive to cut her off precisely at the 60-minute mark with no warning, and in situations that are a little intense, prioritising the welfare of your friend might be the more prudent thing to do. It may not be perfect, but sometimes bending boundaries slightly is far more necessary.

Creating healthy boundaries starts with self-awareness. Our boundaries are how we show ourselves respect and teach others the best way to respect us, so we need to be able to articulate what they should look like. There's no use in expecting other people to respect boundaries that you cannot voice. Communication really is the underrated cheat code to hacking life and all its craziness. Eliminating any potential source of confusion, being bold and clear in setting your boundaries is a great way to lay foundations for a loving relationship with yourself and loving relationships with other people. Note the boundaries, make them plain.

Another part of boundary setting, which is less often considered but almost as equally important, is articulating and doling out healthy consequences for the violation of your boundaries. There is no point in having boundaries if you aren't willing to actually enforce them. Now, this isn't to encourage stonewalling, freezing people out or concocting the most incredible form of punishment you can think of. Having consequences, particularly when you find your boundaries being violated persistently, allows you to shield yourself from harm and other people's irresponsible behaviour. Whilst you can't always change the way that people behave towards you, you can choose whether or not you will tolerate it. Consequences for broken boundaries allow other people to weigh up the cost of violating the terms and conditions of how you'd like to be respected. It teaches others, and yourself, that you can't be stomped over or overlooked. Most importantly, it allows you to make a judgement call on whether or not you want to continue intimate relationships with the people who break them.

Another thing to take into consideration is that boundaries can, and will, change. Change is a function of the human experience and, whether you like to acknowledge it or not, things in your life will not always stay the same. *You* will develop, mature, have new experiences, meet new people – a non-exhaustive list of factors that can contribute greatly to the way you perceive, create and maintain your boundaries. Sometimes, you might experience the changing boundaries of those around you – like the friend who withdraws slightly from you when they've started working a new role, or the friend who starts to open up and relinquish hold of their boundaries after you've spent significant intimate time together. The question is – what happens when boundaries in your life, and the lives of those around you, change drastically?

The first thing you must do is articulate precisely what has changed to the person/people affected, and why and what feelings you have towards these changes. You might have re-embraced your faith, which means different sexual boundaries from those you had in the past. You might have received a promotion, so work now takes up a considerable amount of your time, which means you must be incredibly selective of who you spend your weekends with. You might have had a child, or decided to move abroad, or be suffering from a health condition – there are myriad conditional changes in this unpredictable thing we call life, and both internal and external forces can trigger fundamental shifts in what is acceptable to you.

What makes this even more difficult is when the relationships you have built on a specific set of boundaries are now being pulled up as the people around you struggle to adjust to this new version of you. Sometimes, our familiarity with our friends and sisters can be the enemy of our ever-changing growth journeys. Ever heard of the phrase, 'familiarity breeds contempt'?

When we have close proximity to our friends, we can sometimes develop a sense of entitlement to that person which thwarts their attempts to change. We think that, just because we've been friends for a substantial amount of time, or have gone through specific experiences together, that we'll always be able to claim their time, presence or resources in the same way. *Forever.* It's hard to let your friend be dynamic, especially when you think of them in your life in a very specific way. A fundamental principle to remember when either rolling out new boundaries or trying to navigate new boundaries someone has set you, is to articulate, communicate and adjust.

If you're in a place right now in your life where you must change, upgrade or redraw boundaries, let the people who are closest to you know that you are going through this process. Lovingly inform them that, whilst the mutual bond and love you share will remain intact, its expression may alter due to the changes that are happening. We'd recommend doing this face-to-face, or at least on a video chat to ensure maximum communication and engagement. If you're on the receiving end of new boundaries, express your support and explain that, whilst you may not be perfect in adjusting to the new boundaries, you will make an effort to do so.

It's easy to see changes in a friend's boundaries as rejection or personal attack, or changes in yours as though you're levelling up and leaving people behind. If it's the former, drop the low self-esteem. Seeing your friend enforce new boundaries as a result of good things entering her life needn't be seen as a reflection of how you are doing in yours. If it's the latter, drop the ego. Adjustments do not need to be thought of in terms of your perceived superiority. Sisterhood and community thrive when you choose to see your friends as equal in value. No matter what we do, or what happens to us, all sisters are equal in value and deserve to be treated with respect. If you are trying to build an intimate relationship, or have had one for several years, it is always crucial to assume the best intentions and find appropriate ways to express your effort in making things work between sisters.

ASSUME THE BEST AMIDST THE WORST

Renée

One of my hardest experiences of attempting to enact new boundaries was when I was pursuing higher education. Growing up in a first-generation immigrant family in the noughties in the United Kingdom meant that social mobility was the meal ticket out of poverty. Not to mention that being the eldest daughter meant that I already had to wear a coat of responsibility that was never my size to begin with. I valued education and I loved learning, but there was an ever-present pressure to be the torchbearer for freedom and the poster child for the kid from the diaspora making it out of the hood. To that end, I had finally 'made it'.

In my last two years of sixth form, I took the plunge and applied to Oxford University, despite the fact that no one at my school had ever been successful in securing a place there. Fortunately, I was applying to Oxford at the same time as Courtney was applying to Cambridge, and thus had someone else who kind of understood my experiences, in real time, as they unfolded. Whilst it was great to have Courtney by my side, and the blessing of someone who, right up until and after my masters, could understand what I was going through – quite a few of my other friendships were to change drastically.

It felt as though the moment I received my Oxford offer letter, I was marked. Whilst I was absolutely overjoyed to be accepted, and it was probably one of the defining moments of my life, it started the snowball effect of changes that would ripple across the relationships I held dearest to me. I still remember our last day in sixth form, in the faint British sunlight and summer heat. One of my dearest friends, Rebecca, held a hand over her brow to shade her eyes and looked over at me across the rickety school bench where we were enjoying cupcakes, fruits and other summer treats.

'How do you feel about next year?' she asked, a half-smile on her face.

Rebecca was always an excellent 'reader' – one of those people who can pick up anyone's emotional or mental energy just by being close to them.

I shrugged. 'I'm excited. I don't know what to expect but, we're here now!' I said, offering a half-smile back, to complete the smile.

What was shared between us was missed by our other friends – an understanding and an acknowledgement that things would change. And change, they did.

Things changed drastically from the moment my feet touched the hallowed grounds of Keble College, Oxford. Things changed when I found I couldn't visit my secondary school friends, as I had a 2,000+ word essay to complete every week without fail. Things changed when I started to have extremely difficult, intellectual debates which plucked at my very core beliefs and values. Things started to change when I had to spend weeks applying for spring weeks and internships instead of going on holiday and clubbing with my friends, as that was what Oxford students did.

Things started to change. I started to change.

At first, it was easy to distance myself from my secondary school friends and draw up the walls with no explanation. It was easy to hide behind 'I'm busy' or 'I have an essay' rather than carve out time to realign my boundaries and express myself to my friends. I had erected new time, emotional and mental boundaries – even though no one was the wiser. I would get frustrated when the invites for parties or gatherings would come, and I was swamped with the pressures of university, my degrees, then the whole 'adulting' thing. I assumed they didn't understand and never would – and always silently resented the fact that this was an internal struggle and readjustment period that I would have to bear the burden of.

I withdrew and withdrew, until the days came where my friends checked me on it.

'You've changed, Renée.'

I was perplexed, trying to understand why no one understood that the new boundaries and careful guarding of my time and resources were a direct result of my experiences. How come no one saw what I was going through? How could people only register my withdrawal and not the struggles I was experiencing as I pivoted in the dusty lanes of adulting? Such feedback made it easy for me to assume that these people were not for me or my growth, didn't understand anything about me and certainly did not want the best for me.

It was during one afternoon at Rebecca's house that things started to click for me – still 'the reader', her brow furrowed; she already knew there was something on my mind.

'It just feels like no one knows me or cares much to try,' I wailed. She looked at me with the same half-smile from six years ago.

'You know, it's not that people don't care – everyone loves you, but you've been distant and you need to tell us what's changed about you.'

Courtney, Rebecca and I had a conversation on boundary setting and communication, and what I realised was that as important as it was to have new boundaries to fit in with my life, I was genuinely terrible at communicating them. They just popped up out of nowhere and I relied on the belief that familiarity would allow my friends to understand what I was going through. Amidst my own struggles, I hadn't realised that everyone was equally going through the same changes and erecting new boundaries. Friends were no longer able to go to brunches and lunches so sporadically – financial boundaries and *saving goals were priorities I never knew. Friends were no longer interested in turning up in the clubs as a hot girl anymore – damn, they had partners and children!*

The reality of life is that things will change. When pursuing lifelong sisterhood, what is always important, as my secondary school sisters had demonstrated to me, is doing so together.

Assume the best and articulate the rest – well.

• • •

PUTTING IN THE EFFORT

The importance of communication cannot be understated. When we leave things unsaid, we leave things unresolved. Many of us, due to trauma or life experiences, believe that we must remain quiet, and that those who love us must simply level up or get left behind. Maybe that's something you've experienced, or something you've picked up in response to deep hurt and isolation. But the radical love of sisterhood that we believe in is one that dictates no sister gets left behind. No one is beyond saving and we must try our best to the end. Of course, there are genuine cases where friendships and sisterhood must come to an end. When boundaries have been communicated extensively but are repeatedly violated, then you are well within your rights (and it's in the interest of your wellbeing) to call it a day. But in the same way we are willing to go to the utmost lengths to save our romantic relationships, we must be willing to save our platonic ones too.

Many of us are guilty of assuming. Even though we have personally shared a friendship spanning over a decade, we can assume that, due to familiarity, either one of us will be able to get with the programme. Yet sometimes it's this assumed familiarity with those closest to us that can bring about our greatest downfall. It can at times actually feel easier to put in effort in articulating, implementing and enforcing boundaries with people who are not as close to you. It's those who are around you all the time, or have had the luxury of journeying with you over the span of years, who can sometimes present the greatest challenges when it comes to boundaries and putting in effort. But still, you must try, and still, you must persevere. We must be willing to at least do our best, because the sisters we choose to walk with are worth it.

• • •

SETTING AND ENACTING BOUNDARIES
ACTIVITY

This exercise can be completed alone but for best results, we encourage you to share your process with another sister you trust or are trying to build a relationship with. To get the most out of it, we encourage you to write down the answers to these questions and share them with a friend you feel comfortable enough to do so with.

1. Understanding your values: personal value statement
Before setting boundaries, it is essential to understand your core values. What are the inviolable, fundamental principles that you want to live by, irrespective of what happens in life? How do you choose to live and how do you want to relate to other people? What are the key things you would like to guide your life as you navigate your experiences? These are some of the essential questions you should consider when conjuring up your values.

There are many possible forces that may inform your values, such as:

- Family
- Culture
- Society
- Faith
- Environment
- Ethnicity

Personal value statement writing is necessary as it means you will more easily be able to match up your life expectations, relationships and experiences with what you truly desire. For example, if one of your values highlights the importance of depth and introspection, it's likely you will gravitate towards building deeper relationships, a career that is meaningful to you, hobbies that support growth in these areas, and so on and so forth.

ACTION: Brainstorm or list the things that are important to you. What characteristics, traits, personal qualities and behaviours do you value? We've included a non-exhaustive table of words below to get you started.

Passion	Peace	Faith	Respect	Independence
Love	Determination	Intelligence	Introspection	Honesty
Justice	Security	Loyalty	Wealth	Wisdom
Understanding	Stewardship	Health	Wellbeing	Compassion

- Once you have around twenty words, it's time to start creating themes. For instance, introspection, intelligence and understanding centre around *wisdom*. Security, wealth and stewardship could potentially fit under independence. Try to fit as many words under one specific word theme. Once you've narrowed your list down, pick your top three most important values.

■ Write a sentence on why each of these values are important to you. You'll end up with something like the following:

Wisdom	Wisdom is a core value for me, as being dedicated to wisdom allows me to make better choices and contributions by using knowledge, experience and understanding.
Interdependence	I value interdependence because it allows me to show up for other people, alongside other people showing up for me, in a healthy manner.
Compassion	Compassion is important to me, as it is one of the ways in which we can connect with human beings, and ourselves, in a loving, non-judgemental way.

Once you have your top three values, you can then stack your behaviours and boundaries from this point onwards. We recommend that you keep your personal values statement in a place you can easily access it. You might want to stick it to a bedroom wall or even keep a copy on your phone or laptop. That way, when you are in a tough situation with yourself or another person, you can look to your personal mission statement to provide guidance on how you should act.

2. Defining and creating boundaries

Now that you have a sense of your core personal values, it's time to create boundaries based on your principles. Earlier on in the chapter, we touched on the different types of boundaries:

- Physical
- Emotional
- Intellectual
- Time
- Material

ACTION: Pick one form of boundary from the list above and write down a boundary for each value you have noted.

Let's pick one boundary for this example – time. Many sisters find it difficult to enact time boundaries when it comes to managing their relationships. If we look to the values we have ascertained, we can see we need to create time boundaries that are wise, interdependent and compassionate. They also need to consider our commitments, general capacity and the intended outcome of enacting a boundary.

If I want to be a wise, interdependent, compassionate person, how should I manage my time?

Here's an example:

- Wise: As I am starting a new role, I will ensure that I keep at least three of my evenings free to spend some time resting and recuperating, so that I can show up for my friends.
- Interdependent: I will take turns with my friends to organise how we spend our time together to allow myself and my friends to feel equal ownership over our relationship.
- Compassionate: I will prioritise spending time with my friends on Saturday afternoons and evenings in order to build intimacy with them.

You can repeat this exercise with your values, picking different types of boundaries each time, until you have a full list of boundaries you intend to enact.

3. To what end: creating consequences

A gentle reminder, sis – we don't *want* to send other sisters to the doghouse but it is necessary to be equipped to attach consequences to boundaries that have been violated. It's important that, in being a woman of integrity and a woman of your word, you avoid having a porous boundary in which you create the conditions for the normalisation of violation.

ACTION: For each boundary you have noted, try to think of an appropriate consequence in the event of a violation. Remember, most violations will need to have communication as a fundamental element – you will need to communicate with whoever broke your boundaries in order to give them a shot at redemption. We would recommend a three strikes policy. If you find that they've violated your boundary three times, depending on the severity, you need to book in a conversation and enforce a consequence until efforts are made to reconcile and build up trust again. It's up to you how severe a consequence and how many chances you'd like to give a friend. Some boundaries are more flexible, whilst some may be more rigorous. This is where your values come in – your consequences must also be in line with your key identified values.

Example:

Value	Boundary	Potential violation	Consequence of violation
Wise	As I am starting a new role, I will ensure that I keep at least three of my evenings free to spend some time resting and recuperating, so that I can show up for my friends.	Friends are persistently organising events, calls and catch-ups on days they know I am not free.	I will put my phone on DnD and remove those who violate this boundary from my favourites list. I will schedule a call, or meeting, to inform friends of this change.

You may want to include a minimum adjustment period before implementing consequences, to allow the people in your life the opportunity to get used to the new boundaries. During a season of change, we can often be too quick to dole out consequences without giving people an opportunity to acclimatise. It also means that we can build up a better picture and understanding around whether boundaries are working, and collect necessary data for any persistent boundary violations, before making the decision to go through with consequences.

4. Enacting and reviewing your boundaries

Now here's the exciting part – putting your boundaries to work. You've put in the work to create grounded and well-fleshed-out boundaries, and it's time to see if they actually function as well as you intend. It's all well and good to spend hours putting in the work privately but if they blow away in the wind at any sign of testing you will need to go back to the drawing board. Boundaries are created to be enacted, not remain within the confines of your head, a dusty journal you finally decided to crack open or a really neat-looking computer desktop with a Tumblr-esque backdrop.

Not only must you bring your boundaries to life – you must also review them to see how well they work. Sometimes you need to test them and receive feedback in order to determine the actual (rather than intended) effect. If there is a gap between the actual and intended effect you might have to hit that drawing board again. There's no shame in this. In fact, it's necessary.

ACTION: Pick up to two boundaries you'd like to test this week. If you're reading this chapter, or book, with a friend, you can use them as both a participant and your accountability. As an example, let's use the boundary we outlined earlier on in this exercise:

As I am starting a new role, I will ensure that I keep at least three of my evenings free to spend some time resting and recuperating, so that I can show up for my friends.

Schedule some time in your calendar, or in the next week, to catch up with friends on the evenings that you are free. During the week, make sure to take notes of the following:

- How feasible was it to enact your boundaries? It may have been easier than expected, as you had already accounted for the three evenings that you had chosen. Or perhaps it was harder as your schedule was a bit fuller than you had anticipated.
- What were the blockers that came up? Blockers are anything that may have diminished the effectiveness of your boundary. For example, you may have found that the days you suggested to catch up with your friends didn't work with their schedule.

- Were the blockers 'chronic' or 'acute' (i.e., something that would come up persistently or as a one-off)? In this example, a chronic blocker may have been that the only evenings that work for you are Mondays, Thursdays and Saturdays, which would never work for the majority of your friends due to their working patterns. An acute blocker might have been a family birthday party coming up on one of the days that you were free.

- What response did you receive from others? How did this make you feel? You may have been met with surprise, cooperation, annoyance, sadness and so many more responses, depending on your friends. Make a note of all of these responses and be mindful to note down how this made you feel – particularly around how you may have come across to others.

At the end of the week, it's time to do a self-reflection session to see how it went. This can be either a self-review or a joint review with a friend. Evaluate the impact of these boundaries and whether or not they were conducive to your overall goal. We'd recommend going to a space you really like, if you can. A cafe, a library, outdoors in the garden – anywhere you feel comfortable. If you are with a friend, they may be able to help you answer questions.

Here are some reflective questions to get you both started. You could score each question from 0 to 5, with 0 being poor and 5 being excellent.

Self-reflection questions:
1. *How well did I communicate these new boundaries? Were they clear and fair?*

2. *How well did I implement these boundaries?*
3. *How did implementing these boundaries make me feel?*
4. *How well did my friends react to these new boundaries?*

When you have discussed this with a friend, you may want to think about how to adjust, change or rejig any part of your boundaries. You can repeat this process for the other boundaries you decide to test out throughout the next few weeks.

• • •

BOUNDARIES AND BEYOND

We recommend updating, or at least reviewing, your personal mission statement every 6–12 months. Many things can occur in this timeframe and it's important that whilst you are consistent, you honour the changes that may have occurred in your life that have given rise to new values and priorities. Also, be proactive in seeking feedback for activities three and four in particular. It would be good to get a sense of how well your boundaries are working, whether the assigned consequences are just right and potential areas for improvement. You could have regular self-check-ins on a monthly basis where you journal and review your actions, and we really encourage you to do these sessions with a sister to get an external perspective too. You might even want to host a quarterly check in with a slightly larger group of friends that you trust, including the sisters you are testing new boundaries with, to continue to receive live, ongoing feedback on how well these boundaries are working.

Creating and maintaining healthy boundaries is a necessary prerequisite for your holistic wellness. Far from being a set of arbitrary rules and expectations, boundaries are the means by which we define the parameters of how we operate in a variety of settings and lay out the foundations of what healthy relationships with others look like. Creating boundaries presents us with an opportunity to map out what is important to us, what our limitations are and how we want to be respected by other people. It also gives us an opportunity to morph and change – boundaries can, and should, evolve in tandem with the multifaceted nature of our experiences.

CHAPTER 7

Go-Getters and Go-Get Her

Goal-setting and Accountability

*'Becoming "The It Girl" is not you morphing into
anyone else. It's YOU at the top of your form.'*
COURTNEY

Now, picture this.

It's the morning of 31 December. You've already got plans to celebrate the transition into the new year. Whether it's shucking and jiving at the club, going to a community gathering at a local landmark, having a quiet dinner with family or friends or simply sleeping your way into the new year – you have plans. Yet, whilst you're crystal clear about what you plan to do for the crossover into another year, you have absolutely no idea about the plan for your life. You've attended the women's webinars and workshops on vision casting. You've watched all the YouTube videos on constructing a vision board and still you stare blankly at your canvas – either an actual canvas, your blank laptop screen or the dusty journal you neglected at the start of the current year.

Or perhaps you're a little more hopeful. Perhaps you're excited by the prospect of the *new you*. Irrespective of the year you've had, you see this as the opportunity to start afresh, filled with happiness and hope for a better future. As the days around

Christmas start to run quicker and quicker, you feel ready to articulate the next leg of your vision and come up with the game plan to manifest that vision. It's almost as though you have this palpable feeling that everything is aligning in your favour, and you've already got a list of affirmations prepped for the times ahead. Could this be the time you were waiting for? Could you be on the precipice of finally having THE year you've been dreaming of?

Let's have the conversation on goal-setting and *her* sister, accountability. Because one without the other is much like having crackers without a cup of water – they won't go down well alone. Goal-setting is one of the fundamental aspects of our lives and can form the foundation and parameters around many of the relationships we choose to conduct. Having some form of goals encourages you to equip yourself with a structured plan of action to help you achieve your dreams and vision for your life.

Your vision is what you see at specific points of your life. It isn't what you see when your eyes are open, it's not your present circumstance or projected aspirations. A vision is what you see when your eyes are closed, when you daydream about what your life could be and the prayers and wishes which spark so much joy and excitement in your heart you're afraid to utter them out of fear that you'd have to take a leap of faith to make them happen. Having a vision gives you focus; it gives you a destination for your glowing and growing journey. Your goals serve as your map to these destinations. Without goals, many of us will lack strategy and intentional direction. If that's you, you may find yourself in constant cycles of disappointment, feeling as though you are simply 'going through the motions' and wasting your time on things, people and resources that don't serve you – because you haven't defined what *does*. Now, don't get us wrong. We're not trying to step on your 'go with the flow' energy and of course there are specific periods in which it is necessary to retreat and discover yourself again. However, if this is a hallmark feature of your life, it sounds more like *escapism* from life, rather than an opportunity for rediscovery.

Goal-setting also allows you to create new behavioural patterns and habits which will help you move closer to becoming the kind of person you'd like to be. Once you identify your goals, it becomes easier to break down what kind of traits or characteristics you need to develop, in a given circumstance and timeframe, in order to make it happen. It means you can run a diagnostic of all the current behaviours that are preventing you from thriving. It is through the building up of positive, specific and necessary actions that you get the momentum you need to move towards your vision for your life faster and using the correct means. Furthermore, goal-setting makes it easier to identify what resources you need to make your dreams happen. The process forces us to ask this key question: what time, material and resources do you require to get from A to B?

SETTING GOALS: THE BIG BREAKDOWN

Goal-setting needn't be a difficult concept, but there are quite a few different things you need to understand about it ahead of time. There are many different types of goals you may want to set and it's important you have a fuller scope so you can test out what may work best for you.

The first type of goals are category goals. These are goals which relate to specific themes or areas that we split our lives into and tend to be the most common way many of us conceive of arranging our goals. Here are some of the big ones:

- Career goals: Any aims or intentions around our careers. You may want to work towards a promotion or even get a job at a different company that has alternative benefits. Similarly, you may want to pursue a more managerial role, start a business, become a sole trader or even retire at a certain age.
- Relationship goals: Perhaps the most overused and abused term on social media and the internet alike, relationship goals are the outcomes around how we hope to engage with other people. For example, we may want to go on a holiday with our friends, build a more loving relationship with our siblings or have the goal of marrying our romantic partners.
- Financial goals: Ladies, bring out your purse! You already know that financial goals are centred around the way you use your money or how you earn it.
- Health and fitness goals: Roll call for everyone that has a gym membership and hasn't stepped foot in there! Health and fitness goals are any goals you have which are centred around improving your physiology. This may be aesthetic (around what you look like) or functional (how you move and perform key exercises).

Within your category goals, you may have time specifications. These are typically broken down into short- and long-term goals.

- Short-term goals: Short-term goals have a tighter turnaround time. The exact span of short-term goals can vary, from a week, to a month, to a few months. The bottom line is that these goals tend to have a time frame within the year.

- Long-term goals: Long-term goals tend to stretch over a longer lifespan – anywhere from a year to a few years. These are the big-picture goals – spurred on by classic questions like 'Where do you see yourself in five-plus years?'

We're getting meta here, sisters, stay with us. These goals can further be broken down into process, performance and outcome goals.

- Process goals: Process goals are all about aiming to complete specific actions or performances. For example, a process goal might involve you aiming to read every night before bed for two hours.
- Performance goals: A performance goal is all about improving how well you perform an action. For example, you may aim to run 5km in 30 minutes, rather than 40 minutes. Think optimisation and self-improvement.
- Outcome goals: Outcome goals are all about the finished result. What's the vision you have for yourself after a defined period? For example, you may have the goal of buying a house after five years of continuous saving. The outcome is the house – it's a tangible, finished result at the end of a process.

These breakdowns are important because specificity is the key to success. There are many types of goals and breaking them down into their constituent parts allows you to figure out where you may have strengths and weaknesses. You might be exceptionally strong at executing short-term, process-based goals. However, you might struggle with long-term, outcome goals. It's all about figuring out your weaknesses and making improvements – whilst honouring your strengths and playing up to them.

GOAL-SETTING AND SISTERHOOD

Surely goal-setting is an individual process by which one becomes a better person? It has nothing to do with everyone else and everything to do with you. Well, that's what conventional wisdom would have you believe. In a deeply individualistic world, it's no wonder that such a thread runs through something so innate and personal as goal-setting. We often only begin to think collectively about sisterhood and community when it comes to accountability. We're going to come on to that in just a moment, but whilst many of us enlist the help of friends, spouses, mentors and counterparts to help prop us up and stay accountable to goals we have crafted, we never think to include our loved ones in our goal-setting process, or even think deeply about the ways we could expand our imagination by teaming up. How could you enlarge the picture of success you have envisioned by including a sister or more?

Think about it. How often have you set goals *with* your friends? Alongside them? Have you considered pairing your fitness goals with your friends? Or perhaps buying property with them? Have you considered growing communities or businesses or founda-tions with your friends? Have you thought about going to counselling or therapy sessions with friends, or making goals around increasing intimacy with your friends? This is not to say your life goals should always include a friend but sometimes goals can be made bigger, more compelling and more meaningful when you pursue them together. We set goals as professionals, within the context of our working teams. We set goals with our spouses, in the context of what we hope will be a long-term relationship. Why do we often neglect to set goals with our friends, leveraging the psychological, physical, economic and mental power that comes from community?

A IS FOR ACCOUNTABILITY

Now, moving on to accountability. Accountability is goal-setting's sister; it provides you with the opportunity to take responsibility for your actions, behaviours and movements towards your goals. It means employing the necessary mechanisms and putting systems in place to ensure that you do what you said you would. The term 'accountable' originates from the Latin word *computare*, which means 'to count'. In times past, being accountable meant a person would need to provide 'a count' of either the properties or money they were taking care of. The more descriptive meanings of being accountable, in the sense of 'giving an account', also emerged early in the history of the term. Either way, being accountable means to have something to show for your commitments. It means being a woman of your word.

The world shies away from accountability because the world shies away from responsibility. There are fewer things as scary in this world as realising that you need to take responsibility for the things you do and say. It means that, at some point, you can no longer blame your childhood, your trauma, your heartbreak or anything else for the way you respond. Eventually, what you do becomes a conscious choice.

Rather being a negative thing, sis, we really should embrace the fact that we have free will to make choices. It gives us the freedom and opportunity to build a life that we genuinely want and to be intentional about moving towards those visions that appear to us when we set our goals. Accountability is something that, as women, we haven't always had the gift of in various historical and social contexts. Granted, nowadays it feels as though we are moving too far in the opposite direction with excessive self-scrutiny, but at its essence, accountability provides us with the opportunity to measure how much we match up to the vision of ourselves that we paint.

As a woman, despite the narratives of hyper-independence, the solo boss babe and the 'trust no one' sister, we have several kinds of accountability to tap into.

Mentorship

When we think of mentorship, we might think of slimy old guys, fake friends, cold finger-food and cornering substantially senior workers to hold our hand up to the top of the career ladder. Mentorship doesn't have to exist just in a professional capacity. You could have a mentor in any area of life and, chances are, you probably already do. The point of having a mentor is to have someone in your corner who can offer an expertise you may not have. We use the term 'expertise' because you might find your mentors in some areas are younger or the same age as you. We call this reverse vertical or horizontal mentorship. Mentors are useful when it comes to accountability, as they can provide insights that you may not otherwise get to inform your progression. They can give advice based on their experience and maturity, which is not something everyone can do as an accountability partner.

Seeking mentorship can be daunting, especially if the person you'd like to be your mentor is well-established or intimidating in any way. Our advice is always to be value-driven, empathetic and diligent. Start slowly and get to know the person or people around you who you'd like to mentor you. Offer to be helpful or ask for initial online or in-person conversations around the things that you are passionate about. Focus on building a rapport and a relationship, as mentorship is often something which is offered once a relationship has been established. Of course, there are also a number of programmes and opportunities to look out for if you're seeking mentorship. Lots of local organisations, online and offline communities, and businesses have mentorship programmes for women in various areas. Don't be shy – grab all the opportunities that are relevant to you and maybe explore the ones that require you to put yourself out there just a bit more!

Accountability partnerships

Accountability partners are the most common form of practical accountability we know. They don't necessarily need to be someone who has more expertise than you but they do need to be someone relatively close to you who you can share your progress with. This can be a friend or acquaintance, depending on your level of comfort and how personal your goals are. Accountability partners are great as they can support you, provide a different, external perspective and help you work through obstacles. You can also return the favour and act as an accountability partner.

Community accountability

Community accountability requires you to tap into multiple people and multiple perspectives. There's something beautiful about a shared sense of family and love that can come from community accountability. This can be online or offline, or a mix of both. It's also possible to exist in multiple communities at once. Community accountability may take the form of providing shared updates on goals or opportunities to connect with people within a community to help you with your goals. It's also really empowering to be surrounded by cheerleaders, people who are interested in helping you as they work towards their own goals.

'SHE'S JUST NOT ON MY LEVEL'

We're going to address something a little ugly and that's the reality of dealing with imbalances in ambition and goals. We're all about supporting women and seeing you become the best version of yourself. This is something we address in chapter eight, on comparison and competition. When women are pitted against each other sometimes these two big Cs can be the cause of much heartbreak and lots of resentment. Sometimes in the goal-setting and accountability process, we might hit a wall with our friends because we are so different. There's a couple of different, quite problematic roles that we can play when this happens.

You might be the head honcho – ambitious, witty, smart, intellectual. You have goals that are far reaching and you see yourself as someone who is up and coming. Her goals might be humbler, or perhaps she's just not on the same *level* as you. Sometimes, that's OK. Compatibility is often important in relationships with your friends. However, we need to check ourselves when pride threatens to ruin our friendships. You might perceive yourself, sometimes unintentionally, as better than your friends. Just because their goals are different, or perhaps more conservative than yours, does not warrant a supe-riority complex. This is a teachable moment for you both to come together and appreciate your differences in life perspectives and desires. Sometimes, surrounding ourselves with people who are very much like us, and may be excessively ambitious under the guise of 'healthy competition', can subvert our intentions and redirect our energy towards keeping up with an image or excessive ambition that doesn't need to exist. Be wary of yourself – never look down on the people around you; instead, find ways to leverage your differences to support each other. It is often beneficial to have a friend who is capable of grounding you, who has entirely different levels of ambition, to provide an alternative perspective.

Equally, you may be on the other end of the spectrum. Granted, some women are prideful and exploitative. In this case, it is fair to pull up your close one with love and good intention. However, she may be an ambitious visionary who provokes feelings of insecurity, jealousy or even inadequacy when she shares her goals. Rather than feeling inspired and compelled to help your friend reach her goals, you withdraw, or become decidedly negative or even jealous. If you feel yourself responding in this way, it's important that you acknowledge these feelings when they arise. Rather than allowing them to fester, process these feelings by questioning why you are having them. What threatens you about having an ambitious friend in your midst? Is it that you feel as though, in comparison, you are inadequate? It may just be an opportunity to assess any feelings of insecurity and low self-esteem that have arisen.

Goal-setting and accountability can be incredibly positive experiences. However, sometimes relationships and processes can give rise to ugly things and we must do our best as sisters to confront these when they arise. Rather than burying them deeply and risk them manifesting in what we think are innocent interactions, we must always do the deep soul-searching that leads to their unearthing and our eventual healing.

ENLISTING YOUR DESTINY HELPERS

Renée

'Rise and shine, sunshine!'

That was the sound of Felicity's shrill voice the moment I opened my door. There was something about her that I likened to an oat-milk cappuccino in the morning – exactly what the doctor ordered, and exactly what I needed.

'Your consistency astounds me,' I murmured, rubbing my eyes, trying to bat off sleep. I was normally the morning person amongst us, so it baffled me to be greeted with such cheerfulness from someone who had professed not to be a morning person.

Felicity pushed the door to my room slightly more ajar, and reached over and grabbed my arm, yanking me out the door. The chill of the frosty spring air prickled against my skin, the hairs on my arms standing up. It was the final year of my time at Oxford and it shocked me physically to step outside anywhere that wasn't my room or the library. Spending extended periods of time outdoors was a no-no – we were only a couple of weeks out from finals. It was more typical to see zombie-like students clutching an over-caffeinated beverage and a bursting bag of books walking hastily between their room, and their chosen study space. It certainly was not normal to see anyone so cheery during such a season, and at this time of day.

Felicity jogged on the spot. 'Look, babe, I'm ready!' she motioned, showing me an air squat and laughing loudly. I shook my head incredulously. She was fully kitted out in gym wear – running shoes, all black fit. It was definitely giving gym ninja.

It was just shy of 6 in the morning and we were making our way to the gym. After my newfound dedication to being more physically healthy, Felicity followed suit and we vowed to be each other's keeper when it came to making it to the gym. Felicity was one of the most determined and audacious people I knew. Her college was *roughly 20 minutes away from mine but she had agreed to come to my gym at least twice a week to work out with me and ensure we both got the work done. Good on her, too – I was not about to trek even a minute outside of my college at such hours of the morning.*

'Barcelona calls!' she said, mimicking a salsa movement as I dragged myself behind her to our college gym. We had planned to go on holiday together once our exams had concluded and there's nothing that can get a sister going to the gym more than the promise of wearing tiny clothes amidst sun, sea and sand. Cocktails, cute boys and gelato at every meal. If that wasn't a perfect holiday for me, I wouldn't know what was.

'Girl, I know. I'm not trying to answer but let's get it, I guess,' I laughed. How could I not? Felicity was the kind of woman who had an infectious presence about her. She was the ultimate cheerleader – and perhaps the most insufferable accountability partner I had ever had! She had an easy smile and a light behind her eyes that sparkled more acutely whenever she had one of her bright, mischievous ideas.

'Bikini . . . Barcelona!' she drawled, dragging my arm harder as we approached the door of the gym. I flicked on the light switch and put my water bottle on the side. I could already hear the obnoxious whirring of the treadmill as Felicity started it up, walking with haste. The funny thing about Felicity? She actually wasn't a major gym fan – but her enthusiasm was enough to create the impression that she was. I walked towards her treadmill and cranked up the incline and speed. 'Well, damn!' she said, picking up the pace. I soon hopped on the treadmill beside her, laughing as she tried to tell me one of her questionable jokes at the same time as trying to keep up with the treadmill.

She had encouraged me from my very first year at university, and encouraged me many years later. Felicity encouraged me when I was thinking about pursuing my masters at Harvard. She encouraged me when I left everything behind and took my leave to Massachusetts. She even flew out to visit me for a week, encouraging me to get through the rest of my degree when things were getting difficult. Felicity was there when I started my first real job and sucked at it, and she was one of the first subscribers to my newsletter and my content. She was there during difficult transitions, always pushing me to expand the edges and scope of the goals I set myself. Felicity gave me a standing ovation even when there were no other audience members.

Whenever I shied away from doing things for fear of how big they were, she was adamant that I was the person to get the job done. There were times when she had more faith in me than I had in myself, and for that, I will be forever grateful. It was my priority to return the favour, to see her go from strength to strength in her personal and professional pursuits. It was always a priority for me to stand on the sidelines, cheer the loudest, and ensure that I was there to hold her accountable to that which she had dreamed.

We met up often over coffee, lunch or dinner, and whenever we relayed our goals to one another, it was swiftly followed by 'no, go bigger' or 'stop settling'. There were many times where she sputtered and literally laughed in my face: 'I'm not going to lie, you can do better than that, girl.'

She taught me not only the value of striving towards audacious goals but the importance of believing that I was capable of achieving them.

She was the real embodiment of a destiny helper.

• • •

GET YOUR GOALS, GIRL
ACTIVITY

This segment is all about helping you figure out how to break down your goals.

1. The raison d'être?

Raison d'être is a popular French phrase which means 'reason to be' or 'reason for existence'. Before you make any goals, it's helpful to chart what you exist to do and what your purpose is.

Cue: existential dread.

Now, before you start having heart palpitations, take the pressure off yourself. Your purpose doesn't have to be all-encompassing or over-the-top. Unless you were drafted onto the next set of the *Avengers*, it's OK to have a purpose that doesn't start with 'saving the world from . . .'. It can be something simple, like telling stories or wanting to make an impact in communities you care about. Your purpose operates like a hanger or a keystone. It's a foundational element that everything else will come to rest on.

ACTION: Define a purpose for yourself. Here are some questions to prompt your purpose.

- What do you like doing on a day-to-day basis?
- What are the qualities of the people you care about?
- What do you want your legacy to be after your death?
- What things would you be doing if money and time weren't limiting you?
- What experiences make you come alive?
- What activities, things or people are you passionate about?

This might take some time and several iterations. That's OK – embrace the challenge and take it at your own pace. Also, feel free to evaluate this every year, every five years or even every ten years. As long as you can set a time period and define the scope for your purpose, you're on the right track!

2. 'You da real the MVP': mission and vision to your purpose

Once you have your purpose, you need to define your mission and vision. Use this car analogy.

- Your purpose can be captured by what the car was created to do – to help people get from one place to another.
- Your mission can be captured by the working parts of the car to fulfil that purpose – the engine, the steering wheel, the internal system.
- Your vision can be captured by what you see – a red Ford with blacked-out windows and silver tyres.

Purpose: Why you exist
Mission: How you enact your purpose
Vision: What it looks like when you are fulfilling your purpose

Example:
Purpose: To create and share stories to connect people across the world
Mission: To become a renowned movie director and content creator, creating award-winning content online and for the big screen
Vision: Thousands of people watching and being moved by the stories I create

ACTION: Using the example above, write out your mission and vision statement. You might have a few mission and vision statements, depending on the life category you are focusing on.

3. Making SMART goals

Once you have defined your purpose, mission and vision statements, you need to break these down further into goals. Goals are the specific desired results you aim to achieve, which feed into your mission, vision and purpose. One of our favourite frameworks is the SMART goal acronym, originally developed in 1981 by George T. Doran in his paper, 'There's a S.M.A.R.T. Way to Write Management's Goals and Objectives'.

S is for Specific: Define exactly the outcome you'd like to achieve.

M is for Measurable: How will you measure success?

A is for Achievable: What resourcing will you need to make this achievable?

R is for Relevant: How relevant is it to your purpose, mission and vision?

T is for Time-bound: How much time will you give yourself?

Example:

Purpose: To create and share stories to connect people across the world

Mission: To become a renowned movie director and content creator, creating award-winning content online and on the big screen

Vision: Thousands of people watching and being moved by the stories I create

Goal	Specifics	Measurement of Success	Achievable – what resourcing will I need?	Relevant?	Timeframe
Direct my first movie	I want to direct and release my first movie this year	Complete filming and debut either online or in-person screening	I will need to contact a production team and hire actors. I will need to book screening venues	Directing my first film will help me to tell one of my first meaningful stories	1 year
Become physically healthier	I want to decrease my body fat and increase my strength and endurance	Scales – I will use the scale to track changes in muscle mass and body fat Athletic numbers – I will be able to run for 30 minutes and squat my bodyweight	I will need to get a gym membership and change approach to food shopping	Being fit and healthy will give me the physical capacity to tell meaningful stories for as long as possible	1 year
Increase my income	I want to increase my current income in the next 12 years by 50%	Income level – when my total disposable income after tax and expenses has increased by 50% on average each month	I will need to decrease my monthly spend, find a higher-paying job and build my side hustle	A higher income will help me tell moving stories to communities I care about, as I will be able to spend resources on content	1 year

ACTION: Pick three goals you have for yourself in the next year and fill out this table below. Use the example above to help you.

Goal	Specifics	Measurement of Success	Achievable?	Relevant?	Timeframe

4. Identifying accountability measures

Last (and yet certainly not least) is identifying accountability measures. Who will hold you to what you claim you will do? How will they do it? When will they do it? You can use multiple accountability measures – often, adopting different types of measures will increase your likelihood of success and, realistically, different goals may require different modes of accountability.

ACTION: Using some of the groups featured earlier in the chapter, identify some of the key accountability measures you will be taking to ensure you achieve your goals. Here are some ideas of measures:

- Self-evaluation: Set up regular check-ins (i.e. monthly) where you track your progress towards your goals
- Accountability lunches: Set up recurring accountability lunches with a trusted friend or acquaintance every quarter
- Join specific communities: Post your progress on community boards and spaces

• • •

Being SMART sisters

We recommend doing this full exercise at least once a year. Things change and *you* change, and it's important to build in some wiggle room when life happens and appreciate when you experience personal growth. If you become stuck, or require more ideas, you might want to host this session with a friend or confidante. The SMART goals may be able to help you identify specific actions or resources to help you reach your goals.

Don't be stressed if it takes you some time to establish accountability measures. Many of the measures we outlined are predicated on developing relationships. If you're still in the process of building these relationships, then prioritise that intimacy and connection – the accountability portion can come later! Also, don't forget you can set joint goals with your friends – of course, you may not have the exact same emphasis, but leverage the fact that you can draw on one another to make things happen.

Setting meaningful goals helps bring focus and clarity to your life in an unmatched way. It makes you a better and more intentional person, which will ultimately transform the way you engage in friendships and help you become a better friend to others. Accountability helps you and others invest in the process of growth, within yourself and the people you desire to draw close to you.

CHAPTER 8

Comparison is the Thief of Joy

Navigating Competition and Comparison

'You may not have control over the feeling rising up in you BUT what does the feeling now cause you to do?'
COURTNEY

We've seen so many 'mean girl' tropes played out across our screens. Drama, cat fights and arguments take centre stage in reality TV shows and high school rom-coms. Whilst this entire book exists to illustrate just how beautiful female friendships can be, we are not naïve or ignorant enough to deny that these stereotypes exist for a reason. The ugly side of female friendships is something we have discussed a few times on our platforms and, understandably, it hasn't always been met with the best reaction from people who aren't very familiar with our community and its mission.

Whilst some believe that discussions of this nature add to the negative representation, we believe it's important to not paint women as infallible beings. Like everybody else, we have the capacity to be wrong and to make mistakes – even if we don't see it as such and don't intentionally mean to. We also have the power to inflict pain, cause conflict and display vices as much as we do virtues. It's therefore our responsibility to be aware of these and our duty to minimise them. To ignore these facts would be to render women powerless, denying them the freedom to be imperfect, sensitive and autonomous. It would steal from us the room we need to grow and the grace that should be afforded to us when we get it wrong.

The truth is, none of us get relationships 100 per cent right all the time. Sometimes we stumble, no matter how hard we try. Whether it's saying something you instantly regret during a heated argument, disappointing someone because you didn't follow through on something you said you would or even having a negative thought on a bad day that you wouldn't dare utter aloud, we all make mistakes. What we need to be able to notice within ourselves is when a bad moment turns into a bad habit and evolves into bad patterns and behaviours. If you want your friendships to survive and thrive as your love for each other waters them, you must be on the lookout for the metaphorical 'weeds' that could stifle your personal and relational growth.

THERE ARE WEEDS IN THE GARDEN!

The most common culprits that sprout up to choke the beautiful friendships we've nurtured are comparison and competition. When left unregulated, these can begin to take over our relation-ships, transforming them into something unrecognisable and unenjoyable. Even worse, comparison and competition can morph into a little green-eyed monster called jealousy. Jealousy isn't an emotion we find ourselves falling into overnight. It's a seed that grows by feeding on our insecurities and fears through comparison.

It's normal for us to compare ourselves to other people; it can be instinctual, even. In the animal kingdom, many species size themselves up against their counterparts to prove who is a better mate. But as normal and instinctive as it may be, it is more often than not unhelpful. Don't get it twisted – there is a fine line between healthy competition that pushes us to manifest our greatest potential and competition which is fuelled by a coveting of what others have or what we perceive them to be. That line is so easy to cross and we are often lured towards it by our own fears. Once we step over it, we are led down a dark path of individualism, suspicion and insatiable hunger for more. Jealousy puts a filter on our perspective, causing us to view our sisters as enemies and threats, rather than helpers and companions.

As women, we are constantly bombarded with images and ideals we are supposed to adhere and aspire to. From beauty standards and diet culture to media depictions of what 'femininity' is and is not, we are trained to compare ourselves to each other's looks, weight and behaviour. The insecurity this breeds is capitalised on by many industries, from make-up to fashion and exercise. And alongside this, there is the pressure to be married and a mother by a certain age, meaning we can constantly find ourselves chasing externally motivated goals, seeking to satisfy societal expectations rather than our own unique desires.

If we are coached to internalise that a certain number on the weighing scale and a ring on our finger determines our worth, we navigate life fearful of the consequences of never achieving them by the arbitrary deadlines set for us. We are told we should fear ending up alone, appearing deviant and being left unfulfilled because we 'missed our window', as if joy could only be found in one place and we only had one chance to locate it. To be without these things in our lifetime is to suggest we will have somehow failed in our womanhood. With the existence of such pressure, how can one not become riddled with fear and anxiety?

Anxiety is characterised by excessive worry and hyperarousal, which is often in response to traumatic events. It is a fear that is debilitating and counter-productive, often leaving us crippled, though we desperately desire to make progress. Research has shown that women are twice as likely to deal with anxiety than men. Other research has suggested that women feel more pressure is applied to them by their social networks both on and offline to be in relationships than is applied to men, leading to greater feelings of fear when it comes to being single. Add to this society warning us that we should be listening to the tick-tock of our biological clock and we can find ourselves carrying this terrifying feeling, that we're 'running out of time'. This fear halts us in our quest to discover what we truly desire for ourselves and find true fulfilment. It diverts our attention to the people in proximity to us and specifically their progress towards marriage, becoming parents, buying houses and more. That comparison inevitably leads to us panicking our way towards our goals with worry, anticipation and haste so as to not get left behind, or becoming discouraged by the feeling that we've fallen behind our peers.

Comparison and competition thus become a cycle as there will always be somebody clever, richer, prettier, [insert any other measure of 'success' here] than us, who we aspire to be. Our definition of success becomes how high we find ourselves on an imaginary scoreboard and where we rank against everyone else's performance, rather than the measure of the distance between who we used to be and who we are now. How can we ever find contentment and satisfaction in our own personal development journeys if we are more preoccupied with fighting for a position and ranking than we are invested in our own wellbeing and character? Whilst this 'scoreboard' is metaphorical, the hierarchy it creates is very real and has tangible consequences for women daily. People use our looks, behaviour and achievements to deter-mine whether we are respectable, trapping us on the hamster wheel as we try to run towards approval.

Even if you have managed to unsubscribe from the traditional ideas of what makes a woman successful, the mechanisms of comparison and competition may still be something you have internalised. As more women begin to reclaim their time, living boldly and freely in their own purpose and by their own rules, many of us can find ourselves intimidated by their advances and strides, questioning when and if we too will live as freely and as loudly.

Social media has made it so much easier for us to compare ourselves to each other. No longer do we have to peek over the proverbial fence to see whether our neighbour's grass is greener, now all we need to do is go into our pockets and onto a few apps which show us just how beautiful their lives are. As much as we can tell ourselves that 'the grass isn't always greener on the other side', and that sometimes our neighbour's 'garden' is really just Astroturf, our efforts shouldn't be put towards trying to discredit our neighbour's garden in order to make ourselves feel better, they should be put to use working on watering our own grass.

Whilst it's true that social media is mostly just highlight reels where people showcase their best memories, moments and milestones, most people are not doing this to deceive or incite negative feelings in their followers or audiences. The nature of social media is that we are meant to fill it with content about our lives and the things that we do. Most of us do not desire to showcase the most intimate, vulnerable and private sides of our lives on social media, especially in real time. So we post the things we feel comfortable with people seeing and we believe they'd want to see. Yes, this could be seen as misrepresentation or even misleading, but the responsibility lies with both the creator and the consumer; we as content consumers must be mindful of the fact that social media is not real life. You cannot see a picture or 15-second video of someone and conclude that you have a complete understanding of who they are and what their life is truly like. With such little information, it would be dangerous to compare your full picture with their snapshot. You know what your life is like behind the screen – your childhood experiences, the struggles and successes you've lived through and the different people who play a part in affecting your everyday life. As vibrant, chaotic and multi-layered as your life is, so is the life of the person whose picture or video you're watching and double-tapping. Whilst a picture may speak a thousand words, it takes a lot more than a thousand words to tell the full story.

Social media, of course, has many benefits – without it, we wouldn't be able to connect with sisters globally. However, it also has many drawbacks, as it has introduced new ways for our insecurities and fears to be amplified. Social media provides the tools to partake in a process of comparison. We swipe up and down, consuming image upon image of what other people are doing as a distraction or escape from what we need to be doing. Sometimes it's a harmless break from our daily tasks but when done for long enough, without intentionality, it can cause us to compare what we have and what we lack with those who we think are doing better than us and, to some extent, those who we deem to be doing worse than us. This is nothing new; after all, social media replicates what society is and since we take our behavioural patterns onto these digital platforms, they will reflect the hierarchies and culture we live in offline.

Whilst nature, nurture and social media all play a part in us comparing and competing with others, the outcomes of this comparison and competition vary. We must know how to recognise when we are edging too close to toxicity.

Whilst not ideal, due to the factors we've laid out, we can all find ourselves susceptible to comparison. And although we would rather you not compare yourself to people at all, because as the age-old adage goes, 'Comparison is the thief of joy', it would be unrealistic to think you can get yourself out of the habit overnight.

Sometimes, seeing the progress people around you have made can be the motivation you need. A friend's success in their career may spark in you the desire to go to the next level in your profession or business. Or somebody's weight-loss journey could inspire you to sign up to the gym. To some degree, when someone else's progress causes you to look and reflect on yourself, that is comparison. The result of that reflection could be positive for you. But this easily becomes destructive when the outcome is no longer rooted in inspiration and optimism, but instead your self-worth becomes dependent on 'keeping up' with others. When other people's success fills you with dread and despair about whether or not you too will succeed, it can lead you down a destructive path. Not only is it unproductive but it can pose a threat to the health of our friendships. How do we know we are falling down a slippery slope? Well, let's draw and explore the spectrum and its boundaries.

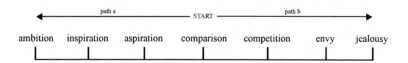

Path A: aspiration – inspiration – ambition

When someone's success causes you to reflect on yourself and your progress, you may compare yourself to the characteristics they display and their achievements. This may lead you to realise that they have brought to fruition something which you desire to see become a reality in your own life. Perhaps you hadn't been exposed to it as a possibility up until then or maybe you simply weren't as focused on that area of your development, but their success or strides set up aspiration and hope in you, helping you to set a goal or vision for an aspect of your life.

Once you've set that goal, the person or image may serve as inspiration to you to keep going in your pursuit of it. If you're flirting with the idea of giving up, or getting distracted, their progress or story may be a reminder that not only is the journey worth completing, it also leads to a good end. You may even be comforted by the fact it has been done before, so it *is* possible. This then takes you to the point of becoming so committed to your own goal and vision that you can find motivation outside of the person who originally inspired it. This is when your ambition transforms from a desire to a discipline; something which you cultivate no matter who is around or on the journey with you. It's easier to take this path in response to comparison when your mind is focused on your own wellness, growth and development above anything else.

When you reach self-motivated ambition, your attention shifts from what's happening around you and instead you invest that energy into what's happening in you. You set your standards according to what you know you are capable of and the potential you're trying to work out of yourself, rather than based on what other people have done. This path is a journey towards self-awareness and self-actualization. It brings you to a point of being internally motivated enough to set your own pace and success indicators in your life; you are no longer living reactively, in response to what other people are doing or social trends. This path requires you to prioritise self-discovery, to find out what you were destined for and connect with what you deeply desire for your life. This is why we emphasise to all the sisters that they need to have a 'vision'.

Often, people who find themselves constantly comparing themselves to others don't have a frame of reference in the form of a vision. So they get distracted by what everyone else is doing, believing it's what they should now do, because they have no structure, guidelines or parameters for how they should live. How can anyone discern what is helpful and productive for their personal journey if they don't know where that journey leads to? This sense of direction helps you to know whose journey you should be taking inspiration from. Your head isn't turned by the winds of culture; instead, you listen and watch other people's stories, advice and content with the intention of finding resources that will bring you closer to becoming the woman you want to be.

Path B: competition – envy – jealousy

This is the more destructive path that comparison can take us down. We can begin to compete with people based on the strides we see them making and the belief that we too should be advancing in the same way and at the same pace. Yes, there *is* such a thing as healthy competition. Usain Bolt, Yohan Blake and Tyson Gay were probably all driven to run faster when they saw each other's performances in the 100-metre sprint across various Olympic races. The competition would've certainly helped each of them push themselves to reach their highest potential as they pursued the title of 'world's fastest man'. But unlike Bolt, Blake and Gay, we do not share a common starting or finishing line. The distance we must each cover in our individual pursuits of success is not universal and the amount of discipline, effort and resources that is required for each of us to cross that ground is not equal. We also do not all have the same obstacles to overcome as we run. If we do not understand or accept these facts, we can find ourselves unnecessarily frustrated by the progress of others in comparison to our own and this can lead to envy.

When we desire what other people have to the point of being obsessed, we can become delusional and ignorant of the process and effort that went into getting it. Without an appreciation and respect for the process, we ultimately become more committed to the materialisation of our desires than the transformation and dedication those goals require from us and produce within us. We can become envious because we believe a person does not 'deserve' what they have because they didn't have to work 'hard' to get it. This could be for one of two reasons, the first of which being that we didn't see the amount of hard work that went into their achievement. When you see a trophy sitting on a mantel, it signifies a personal win, but what you don't see on that trophy is the hours that went into training and preparing in order to get it. Victory can look easy or surmisable when you are unaware of the effort behind it. The second reason is because it *didn't* actually require much 'hard work'. 'Hard work' is relative to every person's individual circumstance. For example, people who grew up with access to different forms of social capital because of their social status or class will find it easier to achieve certain levels of success in their career, finances and education, all of which improves their life chances. This isn't to discredit anybody's achievements; after all, some degree of effort and energy is necessary for any kind of progress to occur. However, we cannot and should not deny that social structures have put us all at less than equal starting points. This is why we must discuss and shine a light on the injustices and inequalities that exist globally.

Whilst you shouldn't be discouraged by other people's progress, sometimes it's hard not to be, especially when you're on your own journey of advancement. It can be frustrating to see people around you already living the life you are still working towards, especially when it looks like it was just handed to them. This is even more true in a society driven by capitalism and individualism, where it truly is 'every man for themselves' because we are often denied help and opportunity by those who have the capacity to give it. If we are to build sisterhood on a political level, we must not only make ourselves aware of the way society's systems place us on unequal ground but we must dedicate ourselves to trying to equalise the playing field across three levels: politically, communally and interpersonally. It is not enough to tell women who have not achieved financial, political or educational freedom and rights to simply work harder; this isn't effective on a global level. We cannot 'boss babe' and 'hustle' our way out of systemic injustice. We also must not chastise women as simply 'envious' when they call us up on our varying degrees of privilege. To do so would suggest that 'personal development' is the solution to institutional and global issues, thus minimising the realities and consequences of injustice, exploitation, war and violence, and absolving us of the responsibility to inspect our participation in these processes.

Jealousy on an interpersonal level, particularly within friend- ships, is dangerous when it leads to dehumanisation and objectification. As human beings, we are much more than just our achievements and our possessions, but when you covet what someone has or is able to do, you reduce them to these things. They are no longer 'the person who can do X, which I admire', they become 'the person who can do X, which I cannot', creating within us a 'me vs them' mindset. This results in us moving beyond viewing that person as a competitor to viewing them as a threat to our pursuit of our goals. This can be rooted in us having a scarcity mindset – the belief that another person's achievement or gain limits our chances of having or doing the same because the thing itself is in low supply. It can also be because we have so firmly attached our self-worth and identity to our achievement of certain things that we cannot let other people enjoy what we do not have yet as it would make us feel worthless. Therefore, we gatekeep access to resources and opportunities which we do not or cannot take up and minimise others' successes, upset that it is not us being celebrated. The further we go down this path, the more we begin to manifest toxic traits such as sabotage, bullying and abusive behaviour in an attempt to exert our superiority or destroy other people's joy and happiness.

TWO GIRLS IN SEPARATE WORLDS

Courtney

In 2015, after graduating, Renée and I pursued two separate paths. She went on to do a master's degree at Harvard University in Boston, USA, and I decided to build my first business in London. Up until this point, we had both been walking side by side in education and succeeding in very similar arenas. It never felt like we were stepping on each other's toes because we considered ourselves to be each other's destiny helpers. We were blessed to be able to depend on each other's knowledge and tenacity for learning and academic achievement as we navigated similar universities, modules, summer schools. We had the same kinds of opportunities coming to us. We were both speakers, content creators and we had been presidents of a university society at the same time. Our lives almost seemed like they were mirroring each other's up until that point.

But after a three-year undergraduate degree, we were faced with the road we had journeyed on splitting into two separate paths. We were up against distance, time difference and packed schedules. We used to see each other every day but now we'd go weeks without a conversation. Like most young adults, we were both facing the struggles that come with transitioning between education and work life, like understanding time and money management, and the unknowns of career development.

Deep down, Renée and I were both being challenged to learn the same lessons, just in different ways. We were so far apart that we couldn't give each other a glance over the table to signal to the other that we were just as scared or frustrated as they were. We couldn't vent to each other on five-hour phone calls at random times of the day because not only did our schedules clash, our responsibilities wouldn't allow for it – we were 'grown ups' now. Whilst we checked in with each other and spent time together when Renée was back in the country during her holidays, it felt like we were experiencing distance in our friendship. We were no longer 'Renée & Courtney', we were 'Renée' and 'Courtney'. We were coming into our own and were obsessed with our own assignments, work and success. We knew that we were still each other's best friends but we embraced the fact our friendship had entered a new and unfamiliar season. We couldn't read into it too much; it was simply that we had been so used to staying in the same nest but now it was time for each of us to spread our wings and fly. We had to live in the hope that we'd always find our way back to each other, because we were sisters.

September 2018 to May 2019 went by like a flash and yet we could feel the tiredness that came with every one of those days. Renée's Harvard degree had come to an end and, just as she had made the journey to Cambridge the previous summer to watch me receive my degree, it was now my turn to finally watch her receive all that she had been working so hard for. I knew the blood, sweat and tears that Renée put into her education. I remembered the day she received admission into Harvard. It was a Friday night and we were at a church event. Her phone pinged with an email notification. Amidst all the excitement and noise in the room, she ran to find me, tapped me on my back when I was mid-song and shouted 'I got in!' into my ear. Our eyes lit up and filled with tears as we gave each other the biggest hug and proceeded to run to the back of the conference room to scream and laugh in sheer disbelief that it was finally happening. That she had once again beat all the odds stacked against her. In that moment, I felt as much relief, joy and pride as she did. I realised that this was my sister, I carried her pain, fears and longings within me, her success was one of my greatest desires. So in that moment, I too had won.

On 4 May 2019 I had the privilege of attending Renée's Oxford graduation with her family. I remember the date because it was also my twenty-second birthday. But I wouldn't have missed that moment for the world. Two weeks later, I flew out to Boston to watch her Harvard graduation. Her mum and I sat side by side during the ceremony measuring how loud everyone else's applauses were as their friends, children and patterns crossed the stage. But best believe Aunty and I were not going to be beat. On the two occasions Renée crossed that stage, we unapologetically shouted at the top of our lungs, garnering the attention of everyone in the room. We have always made sure to celebrate one another loudly! It's one of the pillars of our friendship. No accomplishment, milestone or success goes without praise or attendance because we know how much success means to each of us.

We had never discussed or vocalised to each other any feelings of comparison or competition until we recorded that first 'pilot' episode of 'To My Sisters' back in 2019. It was during that conversation that we touched on how we avoided comparing ourselves over the course of that period and for the first time, we admitted that it had been hard. Both of us had fear and doubts surrounding our decisions to pursue our respective avenues. The idea of either option seemed glamorous and promising but the reality of what it required from us wasn't always a lovely sight. I often questioned whether in setting up my own business, I was in fact copping out of education and rebelling against the corporate world because I feared I wasn't good enough for either. Pursuing either of these two made more sense, carried more prestige and were common among my university peers. I had decided to do something completely different which did not offer guaranteed success and on a daily basis, I just felt like I didn't have a clue what I was doing running a company. On top of this, it seemed like every day my mum would ask me how Renée was and then proceed to ask when I was going to start my master's degree. Little did I know that, across the pond, Renée would be on the phone to her mum who was asking her why she didn't start a business or work after graduation. She was having her own fears surrounding finances and whether it had been the right time to embark on a master's degree. These are the sort of questions that keep you up at night, rattled by the possibility that you had made the wrong decision, that you could fail and that maybe it was all a mistake.

As we sat across from each other telling these stories into the microphone, I couldn't help but be thankful that we had matured so much in ourselves and had developed an appreciation for our own and each other's journeys, so as to not let the very real fear and comparison interfere with our love for each other. I had gone on to build a six-figure company on my own, and Renée had graduated with a whole degree from Harvard, on a scholarship, and was on the road to being one of the greatest changemakers and researchers in the fields of education and business. I was comforted by the fact that

comparison was normal and almost inevitable in our situation,
but that the growth of jealousy was avoidable and we had in fact
succeeded in steering clear from of it. We were both so proud of
ourselves and each other that we realised whilst the rewards didn't
look the same, we had both 'won' in our respective fields. Her wins
were my wins and mine were hers. There was no need to compare
because we were both helping each other cover further ground. We
didn't know it at the time, but we would eventually start TMS
together, where we would combine Renee's research and operational
ability with my creativity and business development skills. It can be so
easy to want to compete when you're really called to complement.

I guess the reason we never brought up our feelings to each other
on the phone was because we self-regulated. We both felt a degree of
isolation and it allowed us to mature and learn to depend on
ourselves as much as we could depend on each other for support and
encouragement. We both recognised this as a personal issue and
challenge. Unfortunately, when we find ourselves getting jealous or
comparing ourselves to other people, we can think that they are the
problem; they're an obstacle in our way, or they're putting their
success in our face too much. If there was one thing we were both sure
of, it was that we were and are destined for greatness. We both pursue
and desire the most excellent of things for ourselves and refuse to settle
for anything less. As soon as we make a goal or desire known to each
other, not only do we take up the role of being each other's cheerleader,
we also assume the position of coach and drill sergeant, reminding one
another of the visions we have. As much as we enjoy each other's
personalities, we honour each other's destinies. You can't be in a
friendship with someone destined to be a star and then be intimidated
by the fact they shine.

• • •

THE SOLUTION

Comparison and competition can creep into our friendships when we least expect it; our insecurities open a window for them to creep in, so we must be vigilant of when we can sense them trespassing in our hearts. As familiar as this feeling may be to you, it's unhealthy. It will steal your joy, crush your hopes and tear your confidence and self-esteem to pieces. It's a weed that literally needs to be pulled out and killed at the root. It is fear. The fear of not being good enough (not only in our own eyes but also according to society's expectations). And fear that if we fail to perform highly, we will no longer be deserving of the love we desire. So, how do we silence the voice of fear in our lives? Well, daily practices like prayer, affirmations, meditation and even therapy can help us confront these deep feelings of despair or worry. But here are some ways to help you reframe your perspective on your journey and success, and create a new culture in your relationships:

1. Embrace your 'seasons'

In the UK, we go through the four seasons of spring, summer, autumn and winter (well, we're supposed to, the constant rain may suggest otherwise). Each season looks different; some we associate with happy times, barbecues in the sun and the nostalgic sounds of ice cream vans. In others, we commit to staying indoors and resting as we hear the raindrops hit our window. No matter which season you love most, each one comes to an end and transitions into a new one. The same is true in our lives. Sometimes we have periods in which we feel like we're experiencing success after success and win after win, like everything is just working out. Other periods of our lives can feel like all we're doing is trying to make things work. Like we're constantly pushing, striving and ploughing to cultivate the fruits of our labour. That's the nature of life; there are seasons when we sow and seasons when we harvest.

Just like with nature, each season may not last the same amount of time and, whilst you may find yourself in one season, it doesn't mean it's being experienced universally. You and your friends may find yourselves walking in two different seasons at the same time. Don't let their time of harvest discourage you in your time of sowing your seeds – your time of harvest will come, be patient and wait for it but don't you dare rip your seeds out of the ground prematurely. What you're growing may take longer to sprout but when it does bloom it will be worth it.

2. Water your grass

Many slip and fall into the trap of jealousy because they are distracted as they walk. As the old African proverb goes, 'Face your front!' In other words, learn to mind your business. Focus on your own journey and the path you need to take. Your vision board is probably full of goals you want to achieve – commit your time and attention to making them a reality. Your to-do list is probably long with things you know you need to do, so make productive use of your time; after all, idle hands are the devil's workshop. Open up your journal and start writing ideas for things that will bring your fullest potential out of you and pursue them. Resist the urge to be distracted, especially when many things are competing for your attention. Comparison is draining; it takes up so much brain and heart space but your flourishing won't happen unless you intentionally and consistently nourish yourself by investing your time, effort and focus into your personal growth and happiness.

Decentre other people's progress from your idea of success. Success is whatever you deem it to be. As daunting as it may seem, challenge yourself to look inwards and ask yourself, 'what do I want for my life?' No matter how contrarian, traditional, simple or extravagant, once you find out what you actually want, make the creation of that life the object your pursuit. Don't just desire it, act on it and make SMART goals to move towards it. Don't just hold your arms wide open to receive what you want, reach your arms out and take it.

3. Ask for help

As destructive as jealousy can be to building a healthy community, you can use the power of leaning on your community to destroy it. Let some people you trust know that it is something that you're dealing with, be vulnerable in revealing your insecurity and allow them to hold you accountable to your transformation. They can help put things into perspective, demystifying the reasons why you believe you should be fearful or worrisome about your progress. It may feel awkward but one thing you should know by now is that we are all about having hard conversations.

If you feel as though people seem to be making progress in certain areas where you keep hitting roadblocks, it may be because they know something that you don't. Simply ask for their help. Ask for information, opportunities and tips on how you too can advance. We cannot afford to be prideful in our friendships. No one knows everything and this is one of the main reasons why we need a diverse community, to help us make up for the gaps in our knowledge as we lean on each other's unique strengths and experiences. Stop trying to navigate your life and personal development alone. Be humble enough to welcome in help for the sake of your own success so that you can go further than you ever could on your own.

4. Celebrate the harvest

Do not become complacent in your friendships. Celebrate and appreciate your friends loudly and purposefully. From birthdays to graduations and new job roles to finally quitting, make your support and love for your sisters known. Be your friend's loudest hype-woman! In a world where we immediately think 'what's next?' after a moment of success, be the reminder your friend needs of how far they have come and surround yourself with people who won't let you forget how far you've come and how well you've done. We can become so riddled with anxiety when we're faced with new challenges, especially when we have forgotten how many battles we have won before.

Even if we have known our friends for decades, have developed the most intimate relationships with each other and have no doubt about the importance of their presence in our lives, we cannot become over-familiar with them and take for granted not only what they add to us but who they are outside of us. We must celebrate their greatness just as loud if not louder than the people who aren't as close to them. We must be inspired by them. The more we appreciate who they are, what they bring to our lives and their presence, and cherish the fact we get the front seat to their victories, the more we realise that to be someone's sister is one of the greatest privileges you could ever have.

LETTER TO MY SISTER
ACTIVITY

We opened this book with a letter to you and now we want you to get out your pen to do some writing of your own. You're going to write two letters, one addressed to yourself and another written to a sister, friend or woman in your life who you've had the privilege of getting close to.

This is something we used to do for each other from time to time, it started as voice notes we would send over WhatsApp on our birthdays. It ended up becoming paragraphs we would send at random times, especially in the year that we were apart. It served as a reminder to ourselves of how much we honoured, respected and believed in each other. It was an opportunity to affirm each other and the dreams we had. It was us letting the other person know: 'I'm here for you, I'm in your corner, your flourishing matters to me and I appreciate the gift of your friendship and presence in my life.'

1. The letter to your sister

Start the letter: *To [insert friend's name]*. And then you're going to tell them whatever comes to your heart. This is your opportunity to celebrate them. Think about:

- How proud of them you are, and why
- What you appreciate about them
- What about them inspires you
- A moment they brought you joy or encouraged you and didn't even know it

Then we want you to think about the dreams they have and affirm them in the fact that they can achieve them.

That's it. Sign it off with your name and feel free to send it or read it to them. The letter doesn't have to be long, it doesn't have to be poetic or profound – it just needs to be honest.

2. The letter to yourself

It may feel strange at first but imagine you were your own friend. Following the same prompts, write a letter to yourself. What are the good things about you, the things you've accomplished and moments you should be proud of? What about your future excites you? Write them down in a letter you keep. Use it as a reminder, especially in moments when you feel tempted to compare yourself to other people, that you are doing amazing, sis.

WHEN THE WEEDS CHOKE OUT THE FLOWERS

You may have done all of these things within yourself and realised it's not you who has the issue. That you've been working on yourself and towards reaching your goals but you've found yourself on the other end of the burning eyes of a green-eyed monster. So, what do you do when your friend is jealous of you? Let's go there.

First of all, be sure that what you are recognising is in fact jealousy and toxicity and not just challenge and disagreement. Some of us make the mistake of perceiving accountability, correction and advice as jealousy. If your friends are honestly giving you productive feedback and you can trust that their hearts are pure towards you, then be sure to inspect why the words or actions have struck a chord with you. Could it be that you didn't like the way they expressed their thoughts; has there been misunderstanding or miscommunication down the line? Decipher whether this is just a bad moment by weighing up your suspicions with their general behaviour towards you. You may need to seek further clarity on things they've done and said just to be sure of the intention behind them before you label them as jealous and take action based on this conclusion. Sometimes these are the challenges we face in our friendships that have to be overcome.

If it is in fact jealousy, realise that it is not your job to fix someone else's character flaws. Do not make yourself smaller or dull your shine, sis. You're not too much, you're just too much for them. Do not feel guilty about your success. Of course, you shouldn't be boastful and arrogant about your achievements, flaunting them in an attempt to make others feel bad about themselves. If you do this, you're at as much risk of losing your friends as you are considering pushing them away. But if this isn't the case, if you're simply being who you are and sharing the moments of your life that matter to you with your friends and yet you can perceive that their reaction to you is negative or backhanded, then remind yourself that it's not about you hiding the good things you have so they don't feel bad. Like we mentioned, comparison, competition and jealousy put a filter on our perception. No matter what happens in your life, if your friend has adopted this perspective, they will process every conversation and social media post as a new piece of evidence in their case against you.

CONFRONTING TOXICITY

Just as with any kind of relationship, friendships can become harmful and toxic when ill feelings fester and bad behaviour goes unconfronted and unaddressed. We all have different feelings towards being 'confrontational'. Some of us avoid it because we consider it to be dramatic or anticipate it to result in more harm than good. The way you confront a person is completely up to you but you must at some point do it. If somebody calls themselves your friend but their actions and words are hurtful to you in some way, you must advocate for yourself by letting them know how you feel and that they must stop. Give them the opportunity to do so and ensure you assess their behaviour afterwards. Do not be afraid to make people confront their own behaviour by telling them exactly what they have done to make you feel how you do. Yes, this may make them feel uncomfortable for a moment but this momentary inconvenience is better than a lifetime of hostility and resentment in you.

Toxicity can manifest itself in different forms within female friendship but a common one is through gossip and bullying. Gossiping especially has become normalised amongst female friends and, whilst we all might like a topic to talk about on a girls' night, when we speak unkindly about our friends and the people we know behind their backs we betray their trust and confidence in us. It can lead to a whirlwind of trouble and consequences, such as the destruction of someone's self-esteem, reputation and openness in relationships. To gossip about someone, bully them or disrespect them is a violation of their dignity and boundaries.

If your boundaries have been violated by someone's toxic behaviour, you are well within your rights to rescind their intimate access to you. No matter how long someone has been friends with you, no one has the right to make you feel unsafe, unappreciated and worthless by abusing you and their position in your life. Confrontation may be their prompt to change or your cue to leave.

WHAT IF I NEED TO CUT MY FRIEND OFF AND END THE RELATIONSHIP?

Friendship break ups are real. Just as with the ending of any kind of relationship, a break up can cause us heartbreak. It can be devastating to lose someone who not only meant so much to you but who you were also once important to. Though sisterhood isn't always easy and it deserves our effort to make it work, that work cannot be one-sided. The success of our friendships is measured by our ability to create an environment where we each feel respected, safe and celebrated – not in an continual and enduring struggle to achieve these things. You cannot be fighting for your friendships, nor can you carry the weight of it alone. The moment your friend decides that they're no longer committed to trying, understanding, reconciling or communicating in your relationship, the friendship is over. Recognise this as the point at which the friendship died, not when you decided to call it quits.

There is no one specific way to end a friendship; sometimes it just looks like putting distance between the two of you and spending less time together. Other times, it looks like having to completely remove someone who poses a danger to you from your life. But when it's clear that the intent is to harm, we are allowed to protect ourselves by revoking people's access to our intimacy and presence. Take time to grieve your friendships if they do end badly. Go through a process of healing from the pain it may have caused you, should you need to. But be encouraged that you have not yet met everyone who is going to love. More sisters are out there and they are finding their way to you.

Sigh it's not the nicest conversation to have, is it?

Having to come to terms with toxicity within you is just as uncomfortable as having to confront it in the people you love. We may be tempted to point the finger after reading this but take time to recognise if you struggle with comparison, competition or even jealousy towards anyone in your life. Don't ignore the weeds growing in the garden; leave them long enough and you'll come back to find that you have no good things left. You may not think it's threatening to your relationships but it sure is a danger to you. We cannot let our insecurities sabotage us by taking away our valuable time, energy and attention from our own goals and future.

We get it, sis, it's hard not to compare yourself to other people. Most of us question whether we are 'enough' and battle with imposter syndrome, wondering whether we are really as good as the people we are surrounded by. We could cheer you on by telling you that you are all these things, that you are indeed good enough and worthy of the good things you have. But our words mean nothing if you don't believe it. Choose to believe that you are worth love, respect and effort, no matter how much society or your life experiences have told you otherwise. We implore you to not only require these things from the people you call friends but to do yourself the honour of showing them to yourself. We dishonour ourselves, our story and our uniqueness when we compare ourselves to other people. No matter how close we are to them, we were not designed to be them and it is when we embrace this that we will reclaim our joy – not in the things we have and have gained, but in the people we have become.

CHAPTER 9

This is Not My Show

Taking a Supporting Role as a Sister

'One thing a sister is going to do? A sister is gonna pull you up on yourself and fight for you to be better.'
COURTNEY

Renée

To me, being a sister means knowing when to add to your joint account or make a withdrawal. Relationships are rarely squarely even. It's a constant process of negotiation. Consider the fluctuation in your bank balance across a year or two. In some seasons, it feels like an abundance. Money is flowing and you have so much to give. Other times, you are in desperate need of your next pay cheque and, in some cases, even require financial assistance to get by. I think this is a great way to conceptualise your friendships. Sometimes your friendship balance will be in the green – sometimes in the red. Sometimes you need to provide more care, assistance and support. Sometimes you will need to be the gracious one willing to lend a helping hand.

One of the most important demonstrators of the highest levels of servitude and kindness and sisterhood was my mother. She was different and born of a time where it was customary to find the greatest ways to serve the people around her. Growing up, my mother not only taught us to go above and beyond for those that we loved but embodied it in every single feasible manner. I have seen countless of my mother's friends at our kitchen table, being comforted with kindness and a hot drink. I witnessed the long hours my mother spent cooking for the events hosted by various aunties and uncles. I have heard my mum rise at five in the morning, praying with such sincerity into the lives of her sisters – some by blood, others by choice. My mother was the first real role model I had when it came to exhibiting true selflessness in sisterhood that I had ever had. But the one season I recall my mother's selflessness in sisterhood shining through?

The story of Aunty Anne

It is typical in many Nigerian families to call family friends 'aunty' and 'uncle' as a mark of respect and age. Such was the case of Aunty Anne, who was actually a friend of my biological aunt. She migrated to the United Kingdom with her partner, Uncle Steve, and their six-year-old daughter. On the outside, to all intents and purposes, everything was perfect. Aunty Anne was always jovial and smiley, greeting me more like a friend and agemate than her cultural niece. She had a distinctive high-pitched voice that sounded like bells whenever she spoke, announcing her arrival and tinkling whenever she left a room. She was small in stature, no more than five feet tall, but her personality could fill a room quite unlike anything I had ever seen before. Uncle Steve seemed to be her perfect match. He was cool, calm and collected – he was rarely without sunglasses, tall and broad-shouldered, with an easy grin and a warm light reflected in his eyes. He was the doting father, obsessed with his little girl. The family seemed to be the kind of family you invite for cookouts, Christmas, birthdays and just round for a good time. There were so many times I would return from secondary school to hear the tinkle of Aunty Anne's laugh or catch the end of a joke Uncle Steve was telling my father. It all seemed so perfect.

It's incredibly unfortunate that images of perfection can prevent us from seeing the holes and gaps just beneath the surface. Almost like a poorly woven tapestry – on one side, you can see an elaborately threaded landscape with vibrant colours and incredibly delicate characters. On the other side, the kinks, loose thread and stitched-over, grievous mistakes are barely noticed once the tapestry is hung. That very much signified Aunty Anne's family. Behind the jovial embraces and tinkling laughs was a world of pain and heartbreak. You couldn't tell from the turtlenecks and long-sleeved shirts Aunty Anne wore that she bore scars and markings after many nights facing a drunken Uncle Steve alone at an ungodly hour. You wouldn't know from Aunty Anne's expensive concealer and powder that she had deep purple eye bags from the exhaustion of working multiple low-income gigs to keep the household going whenever Uncle Steve disappeared for weeks on end. You wouldn't be able to find out from the way she laughed and smiled in the presence of me and my siblings that she spent many a night weeping on the phone to my mother into the early hours of the morning.

In the midst of it all, my mother held Aunty Anne like she had been appointed her legal guardian. When Aunty Anne became pregnant with her third child, my mother spent hours visiting every week, complete with support packages and subsistence for her two daughters. As she was admitted to hospital on the brink of giving birth, it was not Uncle Steve who made it to her side in time but my mother, who held her hand through ten hours of labour.

I remember getting ready for school that morning and walking down the stairs as my mother shuffled back into the house. 'Your Aunty Anne has given birth!' she exclaimed breathlessly, undoubtedly trying to gather herself after an unforeseen overnight visit. My mother held up her hand at me. 'She grips tight! Aunty has had another gorgeous little girl. Guess who's the godmother?' I smiled. I didn't have to guess – in fact, it would've been a little scandalous had my mother not been the only viable option!

My mother went back to help Aunty Anne with her newborn. She constantly bought baby clothes and provisions. She picked up Anne's first daughter from school occasionally. It wasn't uncommon for me to come home from school myself to see Anne's daughter grinning up eagerly at me, her hands covered in something chocolatey or sugary. My siblings and I would take turns entertaining her with games, food and jokes, like she was our youngest sibling.

My mother was the one to call the police when, in the middle of the night, Aunty Anne had finally enough of Uncle Steve during a particularly violent episode. She stayed on the phone with Aunty Anne throughout the ordeal and was present throughout the entire process of finally pressing charges and getting a restraining order on Anne's partner. My mother never failed to offer up a prayer request for Aunty Anne and family whenever the pastor at church beckoned for them. Every single Sunday, without fail, my mum would keenly take up every opportunity to pray for 'Anne and the little ones'.

It's so easy to understand sisterhood and support as something light-hearted, performed through affirmative comments on social media posts, sending a cheeky text or listening to a friend vent for a moment or two. My mother was the first example of true, de-centred and sacrificial sisterhood I had ever seen.

A fear I have is losing such sisterhood – exhibited in my mother, and now in Courtney. A greater fear I have is women I know never finding such depths of servant-like, sacrificial, sisterly love.

• • •

The overwhelming sense of individualism that permeates modern Western culture has been a great asset for many people. As women, reclaiming our agency in so many different arenas has helped us solidify our position in the world as accomplished, authoritative figures, and agents of our own lives. Selfishness can be good. It's important to prioritise the self. A central tenet of patriarchy and our oppression has rested on how much women *should* take care of everything else apart from ourselves. We are told to be subservient daughters, sisters, workers, partners, mothers. We are told to shrink and focus on supporting many things without consciously considering how these things can support us. We have rarely been given the opportunity to take up our place as the leading lady of the day.

And yet now, that's all there is. Sis, isn't it funny how we often fight one extreme with another? In response to decades of iterations of oppressive cultures, we have seen the rise of 'main character' energy and a delight in the acknowledgement of being the champion of our own stories. The heroines. The boss babes. The *it girl*. And rightly so! You deserve to be at the centre of your own narrative; it's a very liberating opportunity to shape what truths you hold dear. Embodying 'main character energy' has unshackled many women from the pressure to appear perfect simply for other people and instead see ourselves as worthy of the limelight. Now, however, all we know are selfies, self-care and self-love.

As revolutionary as it is for women to think about ourselves and remove the implicit or explicit centring of men from our identities and interactions, it means we have also lost a little bit of that sacrificial, deep sense of support and servitude that is necessary for female friendships to thrive. In every main character's story, there is a supporting cast. Life is not a series of endless monologues. Whilst many of us feel so comfortable being the *it girl,* we find that tension can arise when our time to be part of someone else's supporting cast comes along. We find it difficult to find the balance between honouring ourselves and honouring other people – especially when it comes to friendships.

It's complicated. Some of us have conditioned ourselves to take, take and take. We would prefer to be the perpetrator than to be a victim. We lean on our friends excessively, never reciprocating, and manifesting one of the more sinister qualities of the clingy friend when left unchecked – being exploitative. Others resign ourselves to the opposite extreme, where we sacrifice ourselves to the point of resentment because our servitude is not from a place of love. We're always the one who's there for our friends. We're always going above and beyond to show that we are good people. We're always the one appealed to in the heat of desperation. The resentment that this engenders is symptomatic of a fundamental lack of boundaries, a fear of vulnerability and the need to be seen as the 'good friend'. Cue strong friend profile.

We all have flaws. We have all failed as friends at some point. All of us have gotten the whole 'supporting gig' wrong. In that case, let's explore what it really means to be supportive to your friends.

JOINING THE ENSEMBLE CAST

Being a supportive friend means joining the ensemble cast of someone else's life. Have you ever watched a choir perform? Or gone to see a musical? Or perhaps you've watched a Disney movie . . . or four. A show is usually not viable without an ensemble or some form of supporting cast. Supporting cast members allow main characters to shine by providing opportunities for them to show their character through challenging their thoughts, and performing complementary lines and music roles. It's all about enhancement and providing opportunities for the main character to have their moment. Think about this when engaging with your friends – how best can I enable them to shine throughout their life!

In creating 'shine' moments for your friend, you must know what you are working with. Being an active listener and striving to understand them is crucial to this end. You must leave your thoughts and opinions at the door (unless they are welcomed in) and try to be intentional with the information that is being shared with you. Sometimes, when we allow preconceived notions or our own judgements to creep in, we don't fully appreciate our friend for who they are and what they are trying to say. We cut in, interrupt or misjudge what they require from us as we have failed to truly pay attention. As a supporting actor, you must know when to shut up and listen.

It's important to ask clarifying questions and take every opportunity to show empathy and love towards your friend. It's a cruel world out there and usually when your friend needs support, they are looking to be shown something their world currently does not offer them. Think about yourself – when you call a friend or loved one during a difficult time, what you're usually looking for is some form of comfort and love. Its manifestation may be different but the underlying need remains. Let this be your focus when a friend comes to you for support. Ask yourself, *how can I show my friend love and empathy in these situations?* It won't always be so clear what you need to do. You already know that in this sisterhood, we are incredibly big on communication. So don't be afraid to ask your friend what they want from you or how they'd like you to support them. It's a lot more straightforward and means that both of you can avoid resentment later down the line when things are crystal clear.

One of the most crucial things to remember when joining the ensemble cast is to avoid centring yourself. Can you imagine how problematic it would be if one of the buffalos in the background of the *Lion King* suddenly rushed into the centre of the Pridelands as Simba was being presented to the rest of the animals? Or how awkward it would be, in any performance, for an unannounced supporting character to burst into the spotlight? That's how embarrassing it is when you centre yourself! We do it all the time and sometimes unknowingly. In fact, we think that relating someone else's problems to ourselves can be comforting – not always. Have you ever opened up to someone and their initial response was something along the lines of, 'Wow, the same thing happened to me!' All of a sudden, the focus drifts to your shared experiences and the opportunity for support evaporates into air. When a friend is in need of support, whether mental, physical or emotional, try to ensure that, as much as possible, they remain the main character in that story.

Sometimes the support needed is positive. Your friend may be on the brink of breakthrough or may have recently had a major success. Don't diminish this and take it for granted. Our familiarity can be the greatest killer of our friendships – how easy we find it to celebrate strangers more than those who are close to us! Maybe your friend nailed her essay, got a promotion, fell in love, had a baby. When these pivotal moments happen in our lives, support looks like celebration and taking pride in your friend. Let them have their moment to shine in their achieve-ments. Some of us are reluctant to be honest about how much we appreciate praise. Praise your friends – they need encourage-ment. When they win, you win too!

Lastly, and only when requested or necessary, be quick to offer or be a solution in times of need, when it's possible to do so. Your friend may state explicitly that they need support through advice on how to proceed. If they have made it clear that solutions are welcome, then make it a priority to deliver. Also, remember, it's always nice to be kind. If your friend has been having a rough time at work, offer to take her out for lunch to take her mind off it. If your friend has been struggling financially, send her resources that have helped you. If your friend has been trying to improve her health and wellbeing, offer to accompany her to a fitness class. It's all about enacting thought-fulness in order to be supportive.

AN EYE FOR AN EYE?

Establishing balance in support provision can be tricky. As you have been reading this book, you might have identified with several experiences – perhaps being a 'taker' or having a friend who is constantly in a negative balance, or being the ultimate 'giver', or having a friend that violates their boundaries to be saintly. It can be tempting to evaluate support in a transactional manner. This is very dangerous, as it can lead to pent-up resent-ment. You start tracking and tallying how your friends support you and vice versa – only to discover that the maths simply do not add up.

When it comes to support, you must first outline your principles and boundaries. Go back to the exercises at the end of chapter six if you need to. Then, you need to have specific conversations with your friends on the support you may require, the way you like to be loved and how to approach support. You might even want to agree on an informal code of conduct amongst you to achieve some idea of what balance looks like. And, rather than keeping daily tallies, agree on catch-ups interspersed throughout the year to reflect on how things have been going.

If you find yourself in the position of always being the 'taker' and benefitting from the excessive support of your friends, you must reorient your sense of self and start consciously making opportunities to be a better friend. You may also want to diversify your support network. Rather than overburdening one or two close friends, try to make new friends, develop existing weaker ties, and invest in your own capabilities to work through your problems. Your friends should exist as planets in your galaxy and not become your universe.

If you find yourself constantly overburdening yourself to help friends, you must set new boundaries and spend some time creating opportunities to be vulnerable. Chances are, you're prone to overprocessing and are a high-functioning anxious/depressive person, and it is very unhealthy to keep all your problems close to your chest. You are not a burden; you deserve to be loved and supported too.

Don't focus on the miniscule account changes – take a step back and analyse trends and patterns over time. And don't forget to extend grace. You and your friends won't get it right the first time and you certainly won't get it right all the time. Hopefully, you will get to a place where you all feel comfortable withdrawing support and depositing it.

I CAN'T BE YOUR SUN

Being supportive does not mean you must always be the fixer. It's so tempting to want to 'fix' your friends' problems – sometimes by sticking your oar in directly. Let's take a couple of examples.

Your friend might be in a relationship with someone abusive, in which case support becomes extremely difficult. It is tempting to go in all guns blazing to take charge of the situation. *How could I stand by and let my friend suffer abuse?* Or your friend might be addicted to some kind of substance – drugs, alcohol, food, sex. You might be tempted to force them to go cold turkey and nurse them back to full health. Or perhaps it only takes your friend suffering the slightest of inconveniences for you to experience a great temptation to swoop in and be the solution to all their problems. You are ready, able and willing to be someone's *sun*.

Who wouldn't want to be the sun? The sun is crucial to our planet – it drives weather, seasons, climate and makes plant life possible. Without the sun, life on Earth would perish. But we're here to tell you – you cannot be your friend's sun. It fosters unhealthy dependency mechanisms, as well as places false responsibilities on your heart. Providing solutions and being a fixer are two different things. One is complementary, like a supporting character, and honours the choices and freewill of the main character. The other can be antagonistic and, rather than the supporting character, this option is eventually unveiled as a villain.

There will be peculiar situations where your friend will need to depend on you for a season or you will have no choice but to lean on the support of your friends. This is normal and OK – sometimes, when what was once our sun is knocked out of orbit, pre-existing stars must shine brighter to make up the deficit whilst a new sun is born. The key here is to understand that the ultimate goal is independence. If you are relying on a friend for a while, focus on eventually moving towards relying on yourself. For example, let's say you end up living with a friend for a few months after your living situation was made untenable. You might have been kicked out of your house by family, tenants or a spouse. Whilst your friend may open their home to you for a few months for you to crash, do not allow their home to become your home. This complete dependency may occur for a season but you must then actively work towards standing on your own feet once more.

Of course, when things are extremely serious and the support your friend needs is intervention, you must be willing to take that bold step – but not yourself. You may need to get other support systems involved, support systems that are far better equipped to help your friend directly in their time of need. If your friend is in a life-or-death situation and they call you, you better notify the authorities immediately. Or, if they are struggling with addictions or mental health issues, advise them to seek the help of professionals. Sometimes the greatest support we can be to our friends is ensuring they get the help they need from those better qualified to provide it.

You can be a planet in someone's galaxy.

You cannot be their sun.

MUST YOU BREAK YOURSELF?

It's even more difficult to support friends who are dedicated to breaking themselves over and over again. It seems that all of us have that *one* friend who just doesn't seem to take any advice we give or constantly finds herself in drama-fuelled situations. The friend who keeps giving the benefit of the doubt to a no-good, lying, cheating ex-partner. The friend who spends all her cash on frivolous things, only to come and complain about not having enough money and ask to borrow a pound or ten. The friend who doesn't seem take in any feedback on her poor communication skills and how mean she can sound when she speaks. And just before you think you're off the hook – you could be one of these friends, too. You might have already been this kind of friend to someone else, in another season of your life.

How can you offer support when you actually don't agree with your friend's behaviour? Do you continue to offer a listening ear and soothe them despite their consistent poor choices or do you pack a bag and head for the exit? Well, it's often not so black and white, and everyone should be afforded grace time and time again. However, when poor behaviour or choices are made consistently over a long period, it becomes indicative of something greater than 'bad choices' – it is actually a sign of deep character flaws or unaddressed trauma. The friend who continues to entertain an abusive or disloyal ex may have self-esteem issues or a fear of abandonment. This may affect their relationship with you, in time. The friend who is constantly spending money on unnecessary items is frivolous and has a toxic relationship with resources. This may affect their capacity to spend time or resources on, or with you. The friend who is constantly mean and clipped will one day (if they haven't already) used their hot mouth on you. As that's the thing about consistent behaviours – they will show up in other areas, especially within the relationships you hold dear.

When you see a friend making these poor choices over and over again, you must make a decision. It may not end in a total friendship break up and doesn't need to be dramatic. It may just result in a natural drifting or an intentional dissipation of intimacy as there is a lack of compatibility. Support can only go so far, and whilst you can support someone during the building process, it is impossible to support someone dedicated to breaking.

HELP ME OUT: SUPPORTING A SISTER

Being a supportive sister can mean something different to different people. With this exercise, we're going to run through some of the base principles of support, take inventory and actively create some opportunities to be supportive sisters.

1. Taking inventory

Taking inventory means taking the opportunity to figure out what you currently have. It can be super tempting to sit on the extreme of a spectrum. You might believe that you are an amazingly supportive friend or that, conversely, you have an incredible amount of work to do to become a good friend. Typically, most of us lie somewhere in the middle. You might be super supportive and competent in some areas, whilst in others, you have to put in a bit more effort and work to improve. In order to make the most of this exercise, try to picture one or two friends as you assess your strengths and weaknesses. Sometimes, whilst we have some specific strengths in one friendship, we may not consistently bring that quality to our other friendships.

When listing your strengths and weaknesses, remember to frame your weaknesses as something that can be improved. There is no need to be downcast or overly negative about the areas you may be slacking on right now. Shining a light on your weaknesses is meant to help you become better, so don't beat yourself up if you find that you're actually not as great at something as you thought you were. We also encourage you to ask a friend for some feedback on your strengths and weaknesses when it comes to being a supportive friend. This can add colour, dimension and a better understanding of how you engage in these relationships.

ACTION: Create a table, like the one below, in which you can chart your strengths and areas for growth. Below, there is a list of qualities as prompters but remember that these are non-exhaustive – upon reflection, you might find there are more areas you'd like to list down.

My strengths	My weaknesses (areas for growth)

Qualities of a supportive friend:

- Active listener
- Gives time to friends in need
- Shares resources
- Celebrates friends' achievements
- Offers practical advice when needed
- Kind and empathetic
- Quick to be loving
- Encouraging and motivating
- Optimistic about life

You might want to employ a ranking system to make this easier. If you are excellent at a particular quality, rank yourself a 5/5 on that. A quality ranked below 3/5 will need to be placed on the list of areas for growth.

2. The inviolable principles of support

Whether you are starting from scratch, or simply looking for a way to enact and embody being a good friend, we've listed some foundational support principles and some exercises you can practise to help you with your quest towards improvement. We'd recommend testing them with a friend (either each principle with a different friend or all with one – whichever you feel most comfortable with!).

Active listening

So many of us claim to be great listeners but really what we do is hear. Hearing is distinctive from listening. Hearing is passively perceiving sounds, whilst listening means to pay attention to words and sounds you hear in order to interpret their meaning and develop an emotional response. Have you ever been in a lecture whilst playing on your phone, or perhaps played a video in the background whilst you were doing something else? When the lecture or video ends, it's remarkable how little you remember. That's how many of us approach 'listening' to our friends – we hear what they say, perceiving the sounds, but make little conscious effort to interpret the meaning. Listening requires conscious effort, purpose and intent. It means being slow to interrupt and paying attention to what the other person is trying to say.

ACTION: With a friend, take turns to speak to each other for three minutes. When one person is speaking, the other person cannot interrupt. They may acknowledge, laugh or have a visceral reaction. There should not be any other distractions around – so put phones on silent and firmly out of reach – and the speaker shouldn't use any other prompt. Maintain eye contact throughout and pay attention to what they say, as well as any other nonverbal cues. Your friend may speak about anything they feel comfortable about. You can go light – maybe recount your day. Or heavy – talk about a time you felt hurt. The friend must use up the total three minutes. They can pause or end earlier than their allotted time, but the three minutes must be allowed to elapse before you exchange any thoughts or commentary.

After each person has had their opportunity to speak, reflect on the exercise.

- Did three minutes of uninterrupted speaking/listening feel long or short?
- How comfortable or uncomfortable were any of the silences?
- What emotions did you feel as you reflected on what your friend was saying?
- What were your main takeaways from what you heard/ what you said?

Asking the right questions:

Do you ask the right questions when intending to support? Do you ask questions at all? Do you make statements? Or do you even respond? Asking clarifying questions allows you to understand exactly what is being said, whilst asking follow-up questions is a great way to demonstrate genuine interest in what is being shared.

ACTION: Ask a friend to tell you a short story about something that annoyed them in the past, in roughly 60 seconds. Once they are finished, ask them five questions. Each of your questions must begin with one of these openers:

1. *Who*
2. *What*
3. *Why*
4. *How*
5. *When*

The aim of this exercise is to elicit specific details about the story and to try to add depth to what is being shared with you. Often, being able to improve how you give support requires you to demonstrate that you are invested in your friend.

When you have done this, swap and have your friend ask you these questions about a 60-second story you tell. Note down how it feels to have these questions asked of you.

- Did you feel comfortable or uncomfortable providing more details?
- Did you feel comfortable or uncomfortable asking for more details?
- Upon reflection, how could you incorporate these five question starters into your relationships more often?

Emotional intelligence

Understanding and communication is a two-way street. In order to enhance your communication skills, you must be adept at demonstrating and interpreting emotions. Many of us can miss cues or even struggle to perform cues when we have over-rationalised our emotions. It makes it difficult to give support, or receive it, if both parties have no idea how the other is feeling.

ACTION: Write down the following emotions on individual Post-it notes or stickers:

1. *Anger*
2. *Happiness*
3. *Sadness*
4. *Excitement*
5. *Worry*
6. *Surprise*
7. *Confusion*
8. *Indifference*
9. *Fear*
10. *Disgust*

You can add more to make it more interesting if you like. Once you have done this, pick an emotion at random and stick it on the head of your friend. Make sure they don't know what emotion the note says.

Say this sentence (or you can make up your own), expressing the emotion on your friend's head: Hey sis, I really need your support right now. Do you have some time to catch up and talk with me?

Can your friend guess the emotion you are expressing? You can switch between an exaggerated expression and something more subtle to explore the difference. How easy or difficult it is to say this sentence above (or one of your own) to express the emotion?

Intervention or presence?

Part of the difficulty of providing support can be around knowing what type of support to give. To make it easier, we've split the support that can be provided into two main camps – intervention and presence. Intervention is being active – presenting solutions and advice, sharing resources, providing resources. Presence is all about providing the comfort that comes with being a sharer in their life – showing up, actively listening, providing an opportunity for your friend to vent.

ACTION: Write a list of past scenarios with your friend – joyful moments and scary moments alike. Ask your friend explicitly: would you prefer your friends to intervene or to be present? For each, ask them to tell you why. This will give you insight into what you and your friend need, and where there are differences between you. Pay attention to which scenarios require specific responses and how often either intervention or presence comes up. Make a note of them – this will be the guide to both you and your friend should similar situations arise in the future. We'd recommend following up this exercise with a broader discussion about how you'd like to approach support and be supported.

If you found intervention was a response that came up often, this may be indicative of an anxious attachment style or a sign of dependency. If you found presence comes up often, or that you or your friend struggled to articulate what you need, it may be that you lean towards anxious avoidant attachment and hyper independence.

• • •

ENHANCING THE STARS AROUND US

Although we have assumed you are working with one other friend to do these exercises, you can do these exercises in groups of friends too. Try to be open and honest with your reactions and reflections – don't answer with what you think sounds 'right'; answer with what you feel and what you believe your truth to be.

It is just as important to be a part of an ensemble cast as it is to be a main character. We must take care not to neglect our duty to support our sisters in their pursuits, experiences and life exploits. If we believe that life isn't meant to be done alone, then it does not mean simply finding people to hop aboard your ship. Support isn't always passive and it's certainly not always easy. Sometimes it means sacrificing a lot, contending with your own ego or laying aside any pride you've cultivated in your heart. Sometimes it means holding the fort when the foundations are shaking or being an anchor in the eye of a storm. Sometimes it means letting someone else hold the broken shards of your heart in the healing process, and sometimes it means stepping off the podium to let your sister take first place.

Whilst we cannot be the sun for one another, we can enhance how brightly all our stars shine.

CHAPTER 10

The End of the Beginning

Starting Your Sisterhood Journey

*'Sometimes you have to zoom out and take time to perceive
your progress. The best things take a little more time to build.'*
RENÉE

Renée

'So . . . are we really going to do this?'

*I propped myself on my elbows as I had been lying on my stomach
across Courtney's bed. I wiggled my toes under her duvet and gave
her an incredulous look.*

*'Ma chérie,' I drawled, raising my eyebrow with a mischievous
smile. 'It's about time!'*

*It was late October and the blistering winter was starting to pick
up. I was stretched out on Courtney's bed wearing my sleeping bonnet,
an oversized jumper and thick leggings against the cold. Courtney was
dressed similarly, lying directly opposite me, the upper half of her body
propped against her pillow. The sun had set low in the sky – we could
just about see it from the eighth floor, the light bouncing off the blue,
purple and pink of Courtney's headscarf. She stretched over to turn on
the lamp on the side of her bed. How had it gotten dark already? Time
flies when you're having fun – and whenever I was in Courtney's
presence, it felt as though time stood still and yet flew by all at once.*

'I hear it. I've been waiting to do this for a long time.' She smiled. There was an excited spark in her eye and a relieved contentment that comes only when sharing one's innermost thoughts and desires with one who is capable of conceiving of their gravity. I felt the weightiness and the honour wash over me in that instant.

'Thank you for trusting me with this.'

Courtney stretched over to start dismantling the microphones we had hastily attached to the side of her window. It was the only place we could record – my house was far too noisy and jam-packed, and we hadn't yet considered getting a dedicated studio or recording space. We didn't even have a set up or a camera. It was just Courtney and I, sitting cross-legged on her bed, hunched over two microphones just about hanging on to her low window with makeshift clips, wearing our comfiest loungewear. Every twenty minutes or so, we found our reflexes tested, trying to catch one of the microphones as they fell from their precarious spot on the window so we could finish recording.

Our first episode

Courtney and I had been friends for eight years. We'd been through a lot together – the highs, the lows and everything you could possibly imagine in between. Both of us were avid creators and keen speakers. We loved creating communities and telling stories. But it had never really occurred to us to create something together in public – bar a few joint videos on YouTube four years ago, we hadn't taken the conscious step towards sharing the woven fabric of our joint lives to the world.

Courtney and I had sat on many panels and hosted many events in our time. It came with the territory – being online creators and high achievers, we were so passionate about paving the way for those who would come after us, and even for those beside and in front of us. Recently, we were on a panel about being a changemaker by one of our mutual friends. It was on this panel, the moment we had the *lights turned on us, that we knew we had something powerful and something in common.*

Each other.

I listened intently as Courtney shared her story – one of heartbreak, one of torment, one of healing and wholeness, one of great strength and passion. I realised that I was one of the few hallmark constants who had stuck around to see her through to the other side of it all. Equally, as I began to share my own small beginnings and my catapult into the sunshine, I realised that one of my own stars had been Courtney.

No less than 24 hours after that event, we started brainstorming.

'There's just something so powerful about what we share,' she exclaimed on the phone. After spending upwards of two hours talking about our hopes and dreams, our vision for a brighter future and helping the people that needed it most, we stumbled across the secret recipe for our success.

'The sisterhood,' I winked.

Somehow, in the emergence of the independent woman, amidst the rise of the submissive wife and the era of the doting mother, we had left behind one important role we must play: sisters.

Not just those who are related to us by blood but the sisters we intentionally choose and pursue. The deep well of friendship we draw from in the midst of a stormy night. The radiating sense of warmth that arises when you recognise you've been seen by a woman so closely knit with your own soul.

Within a week, we had planned out our podcast. We recorded in bulk at first, especially as we were managing so much – full-time careers, running businesses, creating content, investing in other relationships, focusing on our health. You know, the various tasks and roles that life throws at us. In our first episode, which we had just wrapped up recording that night, we reflected on the genesis of our relationship and used it as a means to dive into the notion of friendship itself. We spoke candidly about our hopes, our fears, our strengths, our insecurities. We thought carefully about what it meant to call ourselves friends and sisters. It was when we finished recording that we realised just how potent this movement could be. It wasn't fully manifest or realised yet, but we had permitted ourselves to dream, and dream big. We spent hours afterwards writing up that vision that has never left us since.

We dream of an expansive community of global sisterhood and friendship.

We dream of a world where a woman is given the opportunity to pursue her best self.

We dream of investing in women's health, happiness and healing.

We dream of you, sis.

And like that, the sisterhood came into being.

To My Sisters was born.

• • •

If you're reading this, congratulations. You've managed to get to the end of the beginning. Or perhaps you've jumped ahead – if so, this is your sign to put down the book, pick it up again and this time, go from the start. You've missed a lot of great food for your soul! It's like starting a three-course meal with dessert – the dessert is extra satisfying once you've been fed that which will fill you up.

Hopefully by this point, you will have laughed, gasped, perhaps even cried a bit, through this little book. Most importantly, we hope that you feel re-energised and motivated to invest in yourself and the women in your life. One of the key messages that has continued to resonate throughout this book is that we are relational human beings, and relationships are necessary to give our worlds depth and meaning. We mean relationships holistically – the relationship you have with yourself and those who are closest to you. We pray that by reading this little number, you will not only have gained a greater understanding of yourself but also a more solid understanding of and framework to use to improve your friendships.

Friendships are multifaceted relationships which we should certainly give more thought and importance to. We occupy a world that can be bleak – full of pain, sorrows, challenges and experiences which may engineer your very downfall. One of the wisest pursuits in the face of such bleakness is to spend time creating and diversifying the support systems we have to ensure that, at the end of the darkest of days, we are equipped to stand in the sun that shines tomorrow.

A study conducted on friendship showed that as we grow older, we adapt to changing circumstances by reserving emotional energy for our most important relationships, with very close friends continuing as central figures in old age. The older we grow, the less capacity we have for creating and maintaining frivolous relationships. Our quest to form and deepen our friend- ships must begin *now*.

AN ODE TO HOPEFUL BEGINNINGS . . .

This book might have given you the tools and principles you need to spark up new friendships. How many of us are so incredibly intimidated by the prospect of reaching out to another woman? We're scared of coming across as desperate, clingy, needy. We're scared of stepping on toes or saying the wrong thing. We've been hurt by so-called friends many times before. Or perhaps it hasn't been on our list of priorities and because we have normalised having few or no friends, reaching out to someone to spark up friendship seems alien. For many of us, the last time we tried to make a bunch of new friends was in school, or when we were thrown into a new environment. Our survival in these environments is often reliant on the people we choose to draw around us. Why do we then deprioritise this in our everyday life? Surely, with the twists and turns and hurdles of life, we need to pluck up more courage to reach out to new people?

This is us granting you the permission you need – make new friends, sis. Reach out to the people you admire and ask them out. Or maybe send them a compliment. Or do something thoughtful. It's almost like courting – except for friends, wink! Take the baby steps. Sure, it isn't foolproof and it's pretty daunting, but we're pretty confident that if you have this guide by your side, you'll be able to start attracting and engaging with women you genuinely want to be around. Not to mention, you'll actually start *becoming* the kind of person that people want to be friends with. It's always a two-way street.

More hopeful beginnings may sprout out of existing ties. Perhaps you have friendships that are in dire need of saving or are on the brink of flatlining. Perhaps you chanced across this book in your last attempt to save something which you thought could not be saved, only to be brought back from the edge of the cliff. Perhaps you've finally decided to give things a go. Much like the relationships we have with romantic partners, we go through the joys and the pains of journeying together with a sister. This quite easily could have been the reminder that the dedication to sisterhood goes beyond a bucket list of demands and expecting other people to adhere to your boundaries. It's a conscious ongoing process of negotiation, growth and empathy.

We strongly encourage you to share this book, or even read this book alongside your best girlfriends. Sometimes it's simply not enough to read and be transformed – share the resource, the experience and the thoughts. Use this as a starting point for transparency and honesty, and prepare to make serious commitments to rejuvenating relationships at breaking point. After all, you owe it to yourself and your sisters to try again.

. . . AND DEALING WITH UNHAPPY ENDINGS

Whilst we are wildly optimistic about the transformative power of sisterhood, we are also realistic. There's a chance that this guide was a bitter pill to swallow, and rather than signifying a hopeful beginning, it confirmed a greater sadness.

The end.

Heartbreak can exist in friendships. You may have realised there are fundamental incompatibilities between you and some of your friends. Or perhaps you have now seen that those you have given the titles 'friend' or 'sister' have not served the function. Or maybe you are already grieving the loss of a friend and this book has helped you to identify where some of the issues were. This is all normal. This chapter of your friendships may not have a happy ending but the overall story still can. There is no codified *way* to end a friendship – much like there is no single approved way to end a romantic relationship. However, there are a couple of things you might want to keep in mind. If you are in the process of, or desiring to, end a friendship gracefully, here are some general pointers:

▪ Give yourself time. Time is often one of the most powerful tools in our arsenal. It can help us process our emotions, transform our perspective and give us the space we need. Before you go all guns blazing to end a friendship, give yourself space to reflect, calm yourself down and articulate exactly what you want to achieve through this break up.

- Schedule in time. If possible, schedule a time to address your friend face to face, or at least over the phone. Ending relationships over text messages can be highly disrespectful and quite curt, and you may want to at least allow your friend the opportunity to share her reflections, if needed.

- Start with the positives. Reflect on the positive moments you have shared with your friend and thank them for their support and any real good they have brought into your life.

- Take accountability for your actions. The worst thing you can do is pretend as though it was all them. Often, we have also fed into toxicity and may have been perpetrators of pain within these relationships.

- Be clear about next steps. How will you progress? Is it a clean break up? Is it a temporary break? Are you asking for some distance and want to be more acquaintances than friends? Be clear about how you feel is best for you both to proceed.

You can't predict or take responsibility for their response. You can, however, be kind, respectful and empathetic, even in the face of a declining relationship. Once the initial break up is done, acknowledge your pain and grieve your loss. You might feel pressed to get out the ice cream and start watching reruns of your favourite films, sis. That is also normal. Some of the friendships we eventually lay to rest are amongst our most pivotal, coming-of-age engagements. Break ups, whatever their nature, will hit us hard. Embrace this truth and take your time before moving on in earnest.

Perhaps, even sadder still, you have realised that *you* were the perpetrator in some of your friendships. Could it be that, to protect your friends from the damage you could continue to cause, you need to withdraw for a period of time? Do *you* need to work on being a better friend and person, rather than fooling yourself and lying to others? It's so difficult to have to employ the clichéd phrase 'it's not you, it's me', but in this case, this entire book may have shone a very stark light on all the problematic qualities and character traits you have done your best to keep under wraps. When you are the perpetrator, you might need to have either a temporary or permanent break up, to work on yourself and become a better person and friend. You must be gracious, kind and accountable in these situations, too.

EMBRACING THE GOOD WITH THE BAD

The journey to betterment will always be complicated. There is a reason why so few of us pursue it in earnest. A great deal of comfort, however, does come from understanding that you aren't wholly good – it means you can have more empathy for people around you who you might have put on unnecessary pedestals. People aren't always good. You aren't either. That's why we must cherish and celebrate all attempts and efforts to consciously walk towards the light. Even more so, when done in agreement, hand in hand, with another person. However, having a practical mindset and understanding human flaws does not mean that we are doomed to poor-quality relationships.

Embracing the good with the bad is more than just a saying – it's how you must perceive and live your life. It's a framework to help you build. Studies have shown that having a more optimistic outlook on life can improve your quality of life and positively influence your mental and physical wellbeing. We need to adopt such optimism when it comes to our closest friends and family. Do you really cherish the good in you and the good in others? Are you optimistic about life and its experiences and opportunities, or do you allow yourself to be consumed by negative coping mechanisms and a downright pessimistic perspective of the world around you?

One of the best ways we can embrace the good with the bad on this journey is through gratitude. Expressing gratitude is a great way to cultivate a more positive mindset, unlock more positive emotions, improve your overall health and build stronger relationships. Gratitude allows you to focus on the good that currently exists in your life. There are a couple of ways you can achieve this. You might want to journal and note down the things you are grateful for on a daily basis. You might go on a walk and meditate on what has made you happy over the past week. You might create a gratitude jar that you add to every so often, so every six to twelve months you can take out the contents and reflect on all the great things that have happened in your life. Life is so fast-paced and so much of what we see online and on social media leaves us feeling like something is missing. Perhaps you just need a means to recognise that the things you needed in life were there all along.

That's how we want you to approach the task of creating close friendships and sisterhood. With an optimistic eye, grace and a bias towards expressing gratitude. Things have not always been perfect and neither have you been – but be grateful for yourself and for the people who you currently have who, in some capacity, have shown up, provided for, supported you, loved you.

Embrace the good.

LEAD WITH KINDNESS

We hate to be the bearer of bad news but it's necessary when it is critical to your growth journey. Life can really suck and that makes people mean. Chances are, you've either been a victim of mean people, have been a perpetrator of meanness or, most likely, both. We get it – between trying to maintain your own upkeep, deal with your trauma, focus on smashing your goals, becoming a better person, making money – a girl gets tired. Heck, you might have read through this book and thought, *'Dang, are you telling me I have all this work to do?'* It gets like that. You know, *overwhelming.* You barely have enough time for yourself as it is. What's the point in committing to doing all of this when the world is already so unkind and unforgiving?

Do you want to know what the secret to happiness is, sis?
Kindness.

Kindness is a type of behaviour that is exhibited through generosity, consideration of others, empathy and concern – without the expectation of anything in return. According to a study conducted on the interrelation between happiness and kindness, people who are kind experience more happiness in life – in fact, the bulk of the happy memories we have are either us being kind to others or others showing kindness to us. If you find yourself constantly feeling unhappy or unfulfilled in your friendships and relationships, we encourage you to examine the exchange of kindness. In what ways have you actively tried to be kind to your friends? In what ways have they shown you kindness? If you struggle to answer either of these questions, perhaps now is the time to start building up your kindness bank account with the friends you already have or the friends you are interested in making.

Kindness is the blueprint to a much happier and much more fulfilled life. In a world that champions individualism, and one which justifies exploitation for gain, it is now more than ever before that the world needs kindness. When everything and everyone else seems dark and mean, this is your opportunity to stand in the sunlight and radiate sunlight. Kindness is a central tenet of sisterhood because kindness is a simple thing that radically transforms us and those around us.

EXAMINE YOUR TRUE INTENTIONS

Starting, fixing and ending friendships is all tough work. Work that requires you to be open and true – to yourself and to other people. In our social media and digital-focused age, the pressure to uphold socially accepted aesthetics and 'looking the part' can quite easily creep into our pursuit of friendships and desire to become a better person. Personal development becomes more about buying pretty journals and posting meaningful quotes on your Instagram than having candid conversations with the people you care about. Female friendships become more about finding women who match your aesthetics and validate every single thing you do. And 'doing you' becomes an obsessive attempt to find the 'right people' amidst a sea of broken relationships – when the common denominator is you.

Building friendship is not an aesthetic exercise or an opportunity to acquire 'cool people' in your life. Friends, much like romantic partners, can be used as trophies and props to validate a shiny made-up life narrative. When looking to build real sisterhood, you must abandon the matching two-piece pink catsuits and expensive brunches – if that is all there is. The issue with props? They're fake. It wasn't designed to perform a function. It was only designed to be seen. Some of us are pursuing friendships that are aesthetically pleasing but leave holes in our hearts because they were never designed to fill them.

Equally, some of us end up searching for friends only in an attempt to fill in the emptiness that exists within us. We look for kind people with gentle natures to exploit them, using their emotional, physical and mental resources, all without any conscious effort to reciprocate. If that is you, it's likely that it's not *just* friends you need but professional help. It is much like trying to build and sustain a house with only a quarter of the materials needed – it's a start, but you'll never be in the position to build something that stands up if you don't acquire more materials. Not just bricks either, as some of you are out there thinking that having *many friends* is the answer to all your problems. You need cement, wood, glass, plastic and a few more bits and bobs if you want to build something that you can live in.

One of the best ways to examine your true intentions is to take stock of your current holistic situation. What is there to gain from the relationships you have now? What do they gain from you, and what do you have to offer other people? It's OK if you have a few occasional imbalances. After all, life throws curveballs and isn't so easy all of the time. However, if you consistently have a conveyor belt of relationships, or you feel as though you are lacking real depth in the interactions with those closest to you, perhaps now is the time to pull in your racing car for some repairs. Establish some new intentions before you begin the process of breaking, mending or starting friendships.

THE 360 HUMAN EXPERIENCE

We've done a bit of a deep dive here – exploring the ways you can find and become better sisters. The focus of this book has been on female friendships but we want to stress that a few of these lessons ought to transcend such neat categories and influence other relationships we have. Ought we not to at least try to mend the broken relationships we have with our mothers, fathers, caregivers, siblings, cousins, mentors and work colleagues? The implications of sisterhood are not simply felt across straight, horizontal lines, but across vertical and diagonal ones too. In the effort to decentre the place of romantic relationships, the male gaze and patriarchy, the work does not stop here. The work starts here, in the challenge to be a better sister, and then a better woman to the other women in your life.

It's important to see the relationships we cultivate in our lives as like a web. Intricate and interconnected, some more prominent than others, some overlapping. Sometimes we can let the false illusion of these relationships as compact, mutually exclusive experiences prevent us from seeing the strength in their connection. Yes, it's difficult. Finding the right balance between relationships, and also *within* relationships, will always pose a challenge. It's like juggling multiple balls at once or trying to stack up a house of cards. But do you know what the key is to mastering both pursuits? Technique. You start with a few well-placed balls, or cards, and ensure they are in the right place or formation. You get comfortable in their stability and their position before adding in additional ones. Sometimes it's not necessary to be a *master* – you just need to ensure you are *good enough*. This is an encouragement for those of us who spend the majority of our time and lives honing in on one particular relationship for much of our time, not realising that, at some point, you must let go of perfection and graduate to a new level of mastery – maturity and complexity.

Let's be radical in our pursuits, then, as we focus on building these platonic relationships. Let's challenge the individualism and predominance of competition that has prevented us from leveraging the beauty of community. Let's learn to love, fully and wholly, the 360 relationships that make up the full human experience.

Renée:

'It was when the coach driver stopped at Milton Keynes, and said we were lost . . . that I also lost it.'

The room erupted with laughter. There were real tears in my eyes, the kind of tears that form when you find something so funny it's like your body needs other outlets to express it.

'To be honest, it was when my glasses snapped in two clean halves, I realised this was not the trip I was destined to take.' Akua snorted, and the laughing intensified.

It was a wintery evening on 24 December, 2017, at our annual girls' Christmas Eve party. It was customary for us to host a girls' gathering every year, in the lead up to Christmas, where we filled ourselves with food, wine and recollections of our funniest moments over the years we'd spent together. After overindulging in rice, chicken wings, macaroni and cheese, freshly baked cakes and other tasty treats, we were all huddled together in our friend Rebecca's living room, the faint sound of RnB classics playing in the background. It wasn't uncommon for us to get a few noise complaints – the girls could be animated in their storytelling and we'd bumped into our fair share of ill-natured neighbours over the past few years.

A couple of the girls were recounting our disastrous trip to visit the rest of our friends who had moved up to Nottingham from London. We had planned the biggest night out – think lots of food, alcohol and partying into the early hours of the morning. However, our night out had taken a turn for the worst – several times. In fact, the entire experience was a sham from top to bottom. It had started with me losing my travel card and almost missing the coach to Nottingham (which I fortunately made in the nick of time), experiencing traffic *which delayed us for over two hours, only to find that our coach driver had gotten lost and had to ask for directions at a petrol station at Milton Keynes. One of our friends, Akua, had broken her glasses and we spent over an hour at the petrol station waiting for a driver who knew where he was going, to replace our misguided friend at the wheel. To make matters worse, our friends in Nottingham were experiencing their own challenges – which included a lost ID and a bout of vehement vomiting.*

It was one of those stories that was so ridiculous, you had to be there. The thing about our girl group? Those kinds of outlandish experiences were exactly our expertise. Not a week could go by without something hilarious happening, which is why we had so much material to reflect on at the Christmas Eve party.

'Doing our makeup in the blue light of the coach was definitely up there in the top five of my worst ever experiences,' Courtney shuddered. 'Did you see those eyebrows? Lord!'

I had the misfortune of trying to take a swig of my wine just as she made that comment and spluttered immediately, 'Nah guys, we have suffered!'

'We actually have the kind of friendship that needs a TV show. Do you remember when we left that fancy restaurant in France on Rebecca's birthday to find a kebab shop down the road?' Akua shook her head. 'Can't take the hood out of the girls!'

'What do you mean? Those kebabs slapped though!' Cindy exclaimed.

The room erupted with laughter again. It was these moments that were so precious to us all. As we had moved from secondary school to university and into the onslaught of adulthood, it became clear to us that the friendship group that had been facilitated by lunch breaks and school discos would crumble in the real world if we weren't intentional about pursuing each other. When the end of secondary school approached, and we were all ready to take our separate paths in life, it initially felt like the end. When we finished university in our respective institutions, having managed to survive the distances and growing pains, it felt like yet another ending. When we saw each other move to other countries, find life partners, get pregnant, experience bereavement, go broke, get rich, get fit, fall into depression, start businesses, end businesses, experience heartbreaks . . . all of these felt like more endings.

I watched the light of the lamps across the living room dance and reflect on the cheery faces of my friends. Far from endings, these experiences had been new beginnings. With each experience, new buds appeared in our garden and blossomed into things that were quite beautiful. Some initially grew into weeds but we had been diligent enough to pluck them out before they could contaminate the entire crop. And here we were, ten years later, eight of us crammed into one of our living rooms for yet another Christmas Eve soiree.

We had such distinctive lives by then. Everyone had various other friends, different family dynamics, other projects to deal with and worry about. And yet, what united us was our dedication to sisterhood and the decision we made a long time ago to honour each other. It wasn't always easy. The girls had had their fair share of cat fights and arguments. We'd even experienced moments where some friends (including myself) had wanted a clean break from the 'drama' associated with girl friendship groups. Especially with a group as large as ours. I still get really strange looks whenever I share the fact that I've got an intimate friendship group of such a size. Once we'd had the opportunity to get over ourselves, we always returned and did the necessary repairs to make it work. We sometimes used our gatherings to discuss the issues that cropped up between us, or the issues that individuals were facing. They were awkward and uncomfortable at first – I mean, who wants to talk about daddy issues over mince pies and Christmas pudding? – but eventually it became part of that intricate relationship we call sisterhood in our neck of the woods. A real sisterhood community.

The Christmas Eve party would always end far too late. The consequence of gisting and a little bit too much of Barefoot pink moscato always meant that we'd finish past an amenable time in the evening. At the ungodly hour of 3am, we'd finally gather our belongings and try to find a way to get everyone home safely. Our laughter would ring like Christmas bells into the quiet night, the air thick with anticipation over the Christmas festivities we were to enjoy at our respective family homes. There'd always be at least two people taking a similar route for safety, and we'd always notify the group chat the moment we were back at our own homes.

The wind was brisk and the cold was biting but I always felt a distinct warmth on my way home. I usually tagged along with Cindy on my way back, since we'd lived so close together for the best part of 15 years.

'Get home safely, babe!' she'd yell as she ducked out of the shared Uber, after giving me a warm embrace.

'You too, Cinderella!' I'd yell back, waving frantically as the car sped off. Within three minutes, I was home. I'd toss my slides to one side and rush up the stairs to my room, slipping into my loungewear and throwing myself inside my bed.

I'm home girls – Merry Christmas! x

I dropped my phone to the side and turned it over. Another Christmas, another year's end, another ending,

Another beginning with my girls.

• • •

Alright folks, show's over! We're packing up and grabbing our belongings to make a gracious exit. Unfortunately for us, but fortunately for you, this is where we sign out. The ship we've been on together for the duration of this book has docked and it looks like it's our time to hop off.

However, the journey keeps going for you.

Now, don't be alarmed. This is not your opportunity to cower somewhere below deck and it's normal to feel the motion sickness coming on – because you're moving forward. This isn't goodbye forever, it's *goodbye for right now.* Our paths will cross again. In fact, we're looking forward to bumping into you and your sisters really soon. Until then, we hope this guide has provided you with insight into yourself and your relationships. Mostly, we hope that you feel empowered and equipped to deal with yourself and your relationships.

We've benefitted from the deep joys and the energising force that is sisterhood. We've been empowered by sisters before us, sisters in our midsts and the sisters that come after us. We've been humbled by a wealth of unimaginable situations and seen both the best and worst in those who we are close to. There have been times when those we have placed our trust in have violated our boundaries and hurt us deeply. There have been times when we've felt the burden of generational pains, cycles and trauma squarely on the weight of our own relationships. There have been a few times when we, too, have wanted to give up in earnest. Through it all, we've been shown incredible amounts of grace, sacrifice and love that we believe you should experience and demonstrate to others.

Our challenge to you is to unpack the full gravity of this little book and seek to enact its actions, principles and advice in your everyday life. In our community, we always encourage our sisters to take the words they consume and reproduce from them.

The fruits we have harvested and share with you provide nourishment, but leave you with a seed – a seed you must now go and plant in, and with, someone else. Our desire is to grow the biggest crop of sisterhood the world has ever seen. One where women feel safe, loved and nurtured to do the most incredible things.

Take the plunge and plant the seeds – let's grow together, sis.

Here's to the end of this beginning.
With love,
Renée and Courtney.

References

Introduction – A Letter to Our Sisters
www.cdc.gov/aging/publications/features/lonely-older-adults.html

www.anapsid.org/cnd/gender/tendfend.html

www.onlinelibrary.wiley.com/doi/abs/10.1111/j.1471-6402.1981.tb00589.x

www.pubmed.ncbi.nlm.nih.gov/10941275/

Chapter 1 – We All Need a Sister, Sis
www.jstor.org/stable/1394725

Chapter 3 – It All Starts With You
www.prnewswire.co.uk/news-releases/personal-development-market-size-worth-56-66-billion-by-2027-grand-view-research-inc-840412806.html

www.dealsonhealth.net/self-improvement-industry-statistics/#:~:text=The%20average%20customer%20in%20the,West%20Coast%20of%20the%20US

www.scripps.org/news_items/6221-do-you-have-superwoman-syndrome

Chapter 8 – Comparison Is the Thief of Joy
www.onlinelibrary.wiley.com/doi/full/10.1002/brb3.497

www.interpersona.psychopen.eu/index.php/interpersona/article/view/6139/6139.pdf

Chapter 9 – This is Not My Show
www.education.nationalgeographic.org/resource/sun

www.psychologytoday.com/gb/blog/happiness-is-state-mind/202107/the-difference-between-hearing-and-listening

Chapter 10 – The End of the Beginning
www.ncbi.nlm.nih.gov/pmc/articles/PMC2894461/

www.ncbi.nlm.nih.gov/pmc/articles/PMC1820947/

www.ncbi.nlm.nih.gov/pmc/articles/PMC6441127/

Acknowledgements

This book is community-oriented work, and it is fitting that we celebrate the community that has greatly impacted and contributed to this. Firstly, we'd like to say thank you to our families. For the love, shared struggles and deep commitment to facilitating our growth in whatever capacity they could. We'd like to express our gratitude to our friends, who have shared experiences, shaped our multifaceted understanding of womanhood, deeply challenged us, and unflinchingly supported us in our times of need. We'd like to thank our editor, Mireille, and the rest of our editorial team – for their commitment to understanding our vision, and being our own destiny helpers in making this a reality. Lastly, we'd like to thank the To My Sisters community. To every sister that has listened to a podcast episode, attended a live show, come on our retreats, or simply has supported us in any way – we salute you, we love, and we acknowledge each and every one of you individually for coming together and always exceeding our expectations of sisterhood.

About the Authors

Renée Kapuku is a creative portfolio entrepreneur, speaker and content creator with a background in education technology, social entrepreneurship and community building. Renée is passionate about gender equality, specifically access to education and financial capital for women across the globe. She is co-founder of To My Sisters, one of the fastest-growing women's development communities, and has worked in edtech, fintech and social impact investment organisations. Renée is also a distinguished writer with a passion for self-growth and productivity. She founded *Optimise Me*, her personal newsletter with over 1000 weekly subscribers, and co-founded the *Phoenix Programme*, an independent writer's programme, powered by AppleBooks and HarperCollins, for young people between the ages of 18 and 25. Renée holds an Ed.M in International Education Policy from Harvard University, where she was a recipient of the Kennedy Scholarship, and a BA in History from the University of Oxford.

Courtney Daniella Boateng is a portfolio entrepreneur, speaker and content creator who is on a mission to use the power of stories, leadership and community for positive impact in the world. Courtney's background in social media and the beauty industry has lead to a convergence in her two passions; women's wellbeing and the sociology of digital spaces. Alongside being the co-founder of To My Sisters, one of the fastest-growing women's development communities, she is the founder of Milk & Honey (formally CDB London), an e-commerce beauty brand and has been listed by *Forbes* as one of '25 Leading Black British Business People to Follow'. She is also a YouTuber and digital content creator, creating weekly lifestyle content for a community of over 100,000 people across her social media platforms, who consider her to be their 'online sister'. Her thought-provoking digital content and candid conversations have been featured on Channel 4 and in publications such as *Elle* and *Teen Vogue*, and has according to *The Times* contributed to the improvement of access and diversity in higher education institutions like the University of Cambridge, where she received her BA and MA in Human, Social and Political Sciences.

To My Sisters

At heart, To My Sisters is the fast-growing digital sisterhood founded to help women across the world draw from the community to manifest their greatest ambitions. Initially founded in 2020 as a podcast, the global sisterhood grew from a few hundred listeners to a community in the hundreds of thousands. Primarily focused on personal development, wellness and fostering positive relationships, To My Sisters is unique in its kind by offering women the space for holistic wellness, growth and healing. From dealing with past trauma to setting up your next business venture, TMS is the one-stop destination for women looking to break the boundaries of what is seen as possible in our time.

Website www.tomysisters.com
YouTube To My Sisters
Instagram @tomysisterhood
TikTok @tomysisterhood
Twitter @tomysisterhood